Interactive SQL
on the AS/400®

Interactive SQL
on the AS/400®

John F. Hovell
Northern Virginia Community College

Prentice-Hall, Englewood Cliffs, New Jersey 07632

Library of Congress Cataloging-in-Publication Data

Hovell, John F.
    Interactive SQL on the AS/400 / John F. Hovell.
        p.   cm.
    Includes bibliographical references and index.
    ISBN 0-13-107186-6
      1. SQL (Computer language) 2. IBM AS/400 (Computer)--Programming.
    3. Database management. 4. Relational databases. I. Title.
    QA76.73.S67H68 1995
    005.75'6--dc20   94-35063
                                                    CIP

Acquisitions editor: *Bill Zobrist*
Editorial/production supervision: *Rick DeLorenzo*
Cover design: *Bruce Kenselaar*
Manufacturing buyers: *Linda Behrens & Lori Bulwin*
Editorial assistant: *Phyllis Morgan*

© 1995 by Prentice-Hall, Inc.
A Simon & Schuster Company
Englewood Cliffs, New Jersey 07632

The author and publisher of this book have used their best efforts in preparing this book. These efforts include the development, research, and testing of the theories and programs to determine their effectiveness. The author and publisher make no warranty of any kind, expressed or implied, with regard to these programs or the documentation contained in this book. The author and publisher shall not be liable in any event for incidental or consequential damages in connection with, or arising out of, the furnishing, performance, or use of these programs.

AS/400 is a registered trademark of International Business Machines Corporation (IBM).

Printed in the United States of America

10 9 8 7 6 5 4 3 2 1

ISBN 0-13-107186-6

PRENTICE-HALL INTERNATIONAL (UK) LIMITED, *London*
PRENTICE-HALL OF AUSTRALIA PTY. LIMITED, *Sydney*
PRENTICE-HALL CANADA INC., *Toronto*
PRENTICE-HALL HISPANOAMERICANA, S.A., *Mexico*
PRENTICE-HALL OF INDIA PRIVATE LIMITED, *New Delhi*
PRENTICE-HALL OF JAPAN, INC., *Tokyo*
SIMON & SCHUSTER ASIA PTE. LTD., *Singapore*
EDITORA PRENTICE-HALL DO BRASIL, LTDA., *Rio de Janeiro*

With love to my wife, Julie,
and my three sons, John, Jason, and Kevin

Contents

Preface

PURPOSE OF THE BOOK

Storing and manipulating data into meaningful information has been the crux of data processing since the first computer program was coded. Today, relational database processing is the predominant approach to storing and manipulating data. Structured query language (SQL), a language designed to empower users of a relational database, is complemented by a machine whose operating system is based on the relational approach to data management—the IBM Application System/400 (AS/400).

The fundamental purpose of this book is to provide an easy-to-read reference on the syntax and use of Interactive SQL on the AS/400. An ancillary purpose is to relate the principles of relational database theory to the practice of data management on the AS/400. Information and direction on the use of AS/400 utilities such as the data file utility (DFU) and Query/400 are included to help the reader recognize the versatile data management capabilities of the AS/400. For the novice AS/400 user, the appendixes include a general introduction to the AS/400 machine.

INTENDED AUDIENCE

This book is intended for both practicing professionals and students. Professionals who work with the AS/400 will find the book a useful reference on how Interactive SQL and supporting utilities may serve their organization's information processing needs. Students learning the concepts of relational database management will find Interactive SQL on the AS/400 an interesting means for learning the principles of relational databases. In general, material is presented so that any AS/400 user may understand how to work with Interactive SQL and realize the potency of the relational database approach to managing data.

SUMMARY OF CONTENTS

The first two chapters introduce the relational database model and define SQL. Chapters 3 through 8 provide details on using Interactive SQL, with examples that may be executed on the AS/400. Chapter 9 introduces Query/400 (an AS/400 utility program that can be used to query a database much in the same way as SQL). Chapter 10 is a practice exercise that provides the reader with a guided, hands-on tour of the material presented throughout the book. Although every effort has been made to ensure the accuracy and completeness of the examples, there is no warranty or guarantee associated with their use.

Throughout the book, database principles (including the relational approach, data models, and types of database languages) are related to the use of Interactive SQL on the AS/400. Appendix A provides an in-depth discussion of normalization, an analysis technique for defining relational database files. For the novice AS/400 user, Appendixes B and C provide general information on the nature and use of the AS/400 machine.

NOTATION

The notation for describing the syntax of the various SQL statements that are presented in this book includes the following:

( )	Parentheses are a required part of many statements.
[ ]	Braces enclose optional parts of a statement. That is, this part of the statement is not necessary.
| |	Bars enclose a selection of choices, one of which must be included.
ABC	Words that are capitalized are required keywords.
abc	Words in lower case are user-defined names.

THANKS

I wish to thank several people for their help and support with this work. Thank you, Marnie Wightman, for your support and assistance in turning the idea for a book into reality. Thank you, Laura McCullough, for your academic encouragement and support. Thank you, Paul Parker and Mark Anderson, for your technical insight and support, which made this book possible. Thank you, Julie, my wife, and Teresa Hovell, my mother, for your patience and for proofreading the manuscript. Thank you, Bill Zobrist, for providing the publishing insight and guidance necessary to complete this work.

John F. Hovell

Interactive SQL
on the AS/400®

1

Relational Database Approach

DATABASE PROCESSING

Computers have been used for decades to process data into meaningful information. The management of data has progressed from making the data an inherent part of a computer program, to creating separate data files, to forming a database.

It is generally agreed that confining data to a specific computer program is far too limiting. The evolutionary step forward to organizing data as separate named collections (i.e., data files) also has proven too restrictive and often ineffective. Today, management of the massive amounts of data that exist is best served by the systematic organization of data into a database.

> ### DEFINITION
> A **database** is a collection of interrelated data stored together to facilitate the integration and sharing of data across applications and among various users.[1]

A database is more than a collection of files that represent one's source data; it is the embodiment of the interrelationships of data that exist to support the processing needs of those who will use the database. There are various ways to organize data into a database. Structured Query Language (SQL) on the IBM Application System/400 (AS/400) machine champions the management of data based on the relational database approach.

THE RELATIONAL MODEL

In the relational database approach, data are stored as a collection of logically related, distinct, two-dimensional tables. Figure 1.1 illustrates a pair of tables that might exist within a relational database called MEDICAL.

D E F I N I T I O N

A **relational database** is a collection of interrelated, unique, two-dimensional tables that facilitate the integration and sharing of data across applications and among various users.

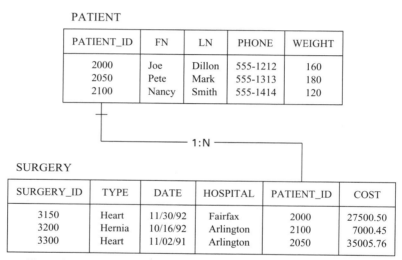

Figure 1.1   MEDICAL Database Composed of Patient Table and Surgery Table

In a landmark paper entitled "A Relational Model of Data for Large Shared Data Banks," E. F. Codd laid the foundation for the relational database approach.[2] His work and writings prior to 1979 formed the basis for the first version of the relational model, referred to as RM/V1. Today, the second version of the relational model (RM/V2) boasts 333 features, which are incorporated into 18 distinct classes that define the relational model for data management.[3]

Unique Tables: Relational Terminology

The distinctive nature of the tables that exist in a relational database is underscored by the term *unique* in our definition of a relational database. In the purest sense, the relational database approach deals with relations, not tables. Relations have a mathematical foundation that sets them apart from typical two-dimensional tables. Let's examine the rudiments of a relation.

Figure 1.2 uses one of the tables from Figure 1.1 to illustrate a relation. A relation is composed of a fixed number of columns (also referred to as attributes). The number of columns defines the degree of the relation. The relation in Figure 1.2 is of degree six. A relation requires a distinct name for each column (for example, SURGERY_ID, TYPE, DATE, HOSPITAL, PATIENT_ID, and COST). The order of the columns within a table is arbitrary. For example, the SURGERY_ID column does not have to be the first column. Nor does any one column have to be physically adjacent to another.

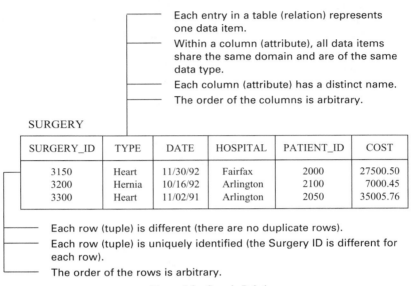

Figure 1.2   Sample Relation

In a relation, all data items within a column come from the same domain and are of the same data type, such as character, integer, or date. Each entry in a relation represents one data item. For example, within the row identified by the SURGERY_ID 3150, only one type of surgery, one date, one hospital name, one patient identification number, and one cost value may exist.

The rows of a relation also have distinctive properties. Each row (also referred to as a tuple) must be unique. That is, no duplicate rows of information are permitted. Each row must be uniquely identifiable; a column (or select group of columns) must be identified as containing key values that uniquely distinguish each row. For example, in Figure 1.2 each row is different and can be uniquely identified based on the SURGERY_ID. As with columns, the order of the rows within a table is arbitrary (for example, the rows do not have to be ordered by SURGERY_ID).

It was noted earlier that all data items within a column come from the same domain. The concept of domain is a cornerstone of the relational model. A domain is a pool of values from which one or more columns may take their actual values.[4] In practice, the concept of a domain is typically achieved by forcing all data items within a column to be of the same data type (such as character, integer, or date).

Although allowing columns to accept only values of a stated data type is a much-practiced means of enforcing the principle of a domain, it only scratches the surface of the domain concept. To explore domain a little further, notice that values for both the surgery TYPE and the name of the HOSPITAL may be character type data, yet their domains are quite different. The domain of the column TYPE includes values that describe the kinds of surgeries that might be performed, such as 'Heart' and 'Hernia.' The domain of the column HOSPITAL includes values that describe the names of hospitals for which data are being kept, such as 'Fairfax' and 'Arlington.'

In some cases the same domain may apply to more than one column. For example, if data were being kept on the mailing zip code for each surgeon and on the mailing zip code for each patient, then two additional columns would be added to the database: one to keep track of the zip codes of surgeons and one to keep track of the zip codes of patients. Although they would be two entirely different columns (and probably in two separate relations), they would share the same domain—all of the recognized postal zip codes.

The relational approach uses many terms of mathematical ancestry, such as *relation, tuple*, and *domain*. It is not entirely inappropriate, however, to refer to the relational model in more common terms. For example, a relation may be referred to as a table, provided that the table abides by certain rules. Table 1.1 lists the rudimentary rules presented in this section.

TABLE 1.1   RUDIMENTARY RULES FOR A RELATIONAL DATABASE TABLE

1. Each column must have a distinct name.
2. Within a column all data items are of the same data type (e.g., character, integer, float).
3. Each entry in a table represents one data item.
4. A column (or select group of columns) must be identified as a key for the table. Each row must be uniquely identified by this key.
5. All rows are distinct; no duplicate rows are allowed.
6. The order of the columns within a table is arbitrary.
7. The order of the rows within a table is arbitrary.

In this text we will consider the term *table* as synonymous with the term *relation*. Table 1.2 maps the relational terms to the more common terms used as synonyms in this book.

TABLE 1.2   RELATIONAL TERMS
AND THEIR SYNONYMS

Relational Term	Practical Synonym
Relation	Table
Attribute	Column
Tuple	Row
Domain	Data Type

Normalization

How does one forge the unique tables that compose a relational database? In his paper "A Relational Model of Data for Large Shared Data Banks," E. F. Codd answered this question by introducing a process called normalization.[5] Normalization is a systematic approach for analyzing interrelated data and storing them as a group of logically related, unique, two-dimensional tables. The normalization process progressively builds a collection of tables of an acceptable form by controlling redundancies and organizing dependencies in data. The normalization process classifies the analysis of data items into tables of first normal form (1NF), second normal form (2NF), third normal form (3NF), Boyce/Codd normal form (BCNF), fourth normal form (4NF), and fifth normal form (5NF). As a table is organized to meet specified conditions, it progresses from 1NF to 5NF. (These conditions are described in detail in Appendix A.)

Let us consider how a table is normalized to 2NF form. The unnormalized table, Table 1 in Figure 1.3, contains data on patients and the surgeries that they have undergone. The table is two-dimensional in nature, but is not appropriate for inclusion in a relational database. If only the PATIENT_ID column value is used to identify each row of the table (proposed keys are underlined in the figure), the row for PATIENT_ID 2000 will have multiple entries in some column positions because John Doe has undergone two surgeries.

Table 2 of Figure 1.3 proposes a solution to this problem; it eliminates multiple entries in a row by repeating the patient data for each surgery performed (that is, John Doe's ID, name, and phone number are repeated for each surgery he has undergone), thus creating new rows. But now the table violates the relational rule that each row must be uniquely identified because both rows for John Doe are identified by the same PATIENT_ID value.

In normalization terms, this is a problem of repeating groups. To remove the repeating groups and advance the table from unnormalized form to 1NF, we can simply propose a collection of columns (called a candidate key) that, when referenced together, will uniquely identify each row. Table 3 of Figure 1.3 illustrates how 1NF is achieved in our example—the combination of PATIENT_ID + SURGERY_ID is used as the candidate key.

Having achieved 1NF, we now must examine our table for partial key dependencies. That is, for any of the columns that are not a part of our candidate key, are all of the elements of the key really required to identify the column, or do we need only a part of the key? In Table 3 of Figure 1.3, for example, we do not need the SURGERY_ID to identify a patient's name and phone number. Knowing only the PATIENT_ID is enough to lead us to the patient's name and phone number. Thus, each of the columns FN, LN, and PHONE only depends on one part of the candidate key—the PATIENT_ID.

By removing those columns with partial key dependencies and placing them in a separate table with the part of the key that best identifies them, we move from 1NF to 2NF. Figure 1.3 advances our example to 2NF by creating two tables, Tables 4a and 4b. Note that the example retains the PATIENT_ID in the second table, but that only the SURGERY_ID is identified as the candidate key in the second table. The PATIENT_ID in the second table is called a foreign key (see the discussion of keys later in this chapter).

TABLE 1   UNNORMALIZED TABLE

PATIENT_ID	FN	LN	PHONE	SURGERY_ID	TYPE	DATE	HOSPITAL	COST
1000	Mary	Jones	555-1111	9010	Cosmetic	10/12/91	Arlington	6000
2000	John	Doe	555-2222	9000	Heart	12/12/90	Fairfax	20000
				9020	Brain	11/11/92	Fairfax	30000
3000	Peter	Smith	555-3333	9030	Cosmetic	11/15/92	Arlington	6000

Note: Assume that PATIENT_ID alone is used to identify each row of the table.

TABLE 2   FLAT BUT STILL UNNORMALIZED TABLE

PATIENT_ID	FN	LN	PHONE	SURGERY_ID	TYPE	DATE	HOSPITAL	COST
1000	Mary	Jones	555-1111	9010	Cosmetic	10/12/91	Arlington	6000
2000	John	Doe	555-2222	9000	Heart	12/12/90	Fairfax	20000
2000	John	Doe	555-2222	9020	Brain	11/11/92	Fairfax	30000
3000	Peter	Smith	555-3333	9030	Cosmetic	11/15/92	Arlington	6000

Note: Assume that PATIENT_ID alone is used to identify each row of the table.

TABLE 3   FIRST NORMAL FORM TABLE

PATIENT_ID	FN	LN	PHONE	SURGERY_ID	TYPE	DATE	HOSPITAL	COST
1000	Mary	Jones	555-1111	9010	Cosmetic	10/12/91	Arlington	6000
2000	John	Doe	555-2222	9000	Heart	12/12/90	Fairfax	20000
2000	John	Doe	555-2222	9020	Brain	11/11/92	Fairfax	30000
3000	Peter	Smith	555-3333	9030	Cosmetic	11/15/92	Arlington	6000

Note: PATIENT_ID and SURGERY_ID together uniquely identify each row and collectively represent the candidate key.

TABLE 4a   SECOND NORMAL FORM TABLE

PATIENT_ID	FN	LN	PHONE
1000	Mary	Jones	555-1111
2000	John	Doe	555-2222
3000	Peter	Smith	555-3333

TABLE 4b   SECOND NORMAL FORM TABLE

SURGERY_ID	TYPE	DATE	HOSPITAL	COST	PATIENT_ID
9010	Cosmetic	10/12/91	Arlington	6000	1000
9000	Heart	12/12/90	Fairfax	20000	2000
9020	Brain	11/11/92	Fairfax	30000	2000
9030	Cosmetic	11/15/92	Arlington	6000	3000

Figure 1.3   Normalization Example

Note: Underlining indicates a proposed key field.

It is generally agreed that 3NF is the minimum acceptable form for a collection of tables representing a relational database. Tables 4 and 4b in Figure 1.3 not only qualify for 2NF, but also pass the test for 3NF. The interested reader is referred to Appendix A for an explanation of the 3NF test and for more details on the normalization process.

Types of Relationships

An intrinsic part of the database approach to managing data is relating one data entity to another. A data entity is something that has meaning to the user. It could describe a person, place, or thing. Understanding the types of relationships that can exist among data entities is a prerequisite to appreciating the concept of storing interrelated data together in a database.

DEFINITION

A **relationship** is the association of one entity to another. Three types of relationships exist:

1. one to one,
2. one to many, and
3. many to many.

A one-to-one relationship exists when, for every value representing one entity, there is a single corresponding value representing another entity. Consider the relationship between airline tickets and seats on an airplane:

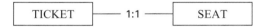

The preceding diagram suggests that for every airline ticket there exists a single corresponding seat on the airplane. Drawing a line between the two entities indicates the existence of a one-to-one (1:1) relationship between the two entities. To be explicit, we have labeled the line 1:1.

A one-to-many (1:N) or many-to-one (N:1) relationship exists when, for every value representing one entity, there may be zero, one, or many values representing another entity. Consider the diagram in Figure 1.4, which enlarges our previous medical database example. The diagram indicates that a one-to-many relationship exists between a patient and surgeries performed. That is, a patient may have zero, one, or many surgeries, but each surgery has only one patient.

The one-to-many relationship is identified in Figure 1.4 by labeling the line 1:N. The dash on the connecting line under the PATIENT entity indicates that if a value in the SURGERY entity exists, then there must be a corresponding PATIENT entity (no surgery takes place without a patient!).

A many-to-many (N:M) relationship exists when, for either entity, a value representing one entity may have zero, one, or many values representing the other entity. A many-to-many relationship is identified in Figure 1.4 between DOCTOR and PATIENT because a doctor may have many patients and a patient may have many doctors.

The diagram in Figure 1.4 is referred to as an entity relationship diagram, as it depicts relevant medical entities and their relationships to one another. It is important to note that the entities do not directly correspond to tables. The astute reader has surely ascertained this by recalling that two of the basic rules of the relational approach are that no table can contain duplicate rows and that, in a given row, multiple values within a column are not allowed.

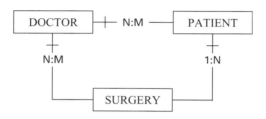

Figure 1.4 Medical Entities and Their Relationships

If we considered each entity in Figure 1.4 to be a table, then we would have a problem in representing the relationship between patients and doctors. The relationship could not be accounted for by including in the PATIENT table a column that identified the relevant surgeons, because in some cases we would be entering a single value, but in other cases we would want to enter two or more doctor identification values for those patients who visited more than one doctor. The same argument holds for including a column for storing patient identification values in the DOCTOR table.

In general, N:M relationships are supported in the relational approach by decomposition into 1:N relationships. The additional structure required to represent the intersection of the two N:M related tables is referred to as an intersection table. The relational database structure depicted in Figure 1.5 includes the intersection table DOCPAT, to account for the many-to-many relationships between doctors and patients, and the intersection table DOCSUR, for the relationships between doctors and surgeries performed. Note that the columns of an intersection table are those columns that were identified as composing the primary key of the two relations involved. The normalization process typically results in the identification of intersection tables.

It is important to note that the relationships that exist in a relational database are carried within the data. There are no separate structures used to represent how one data item refers to another. For example, in our MEDICAL database depicted in Figure 1.1 only two structures exist: one representing the PATIENT table and one representing the SURGERY table. There is no additional, separate structure that is drawn (or later created in the database) to account for the relationship between the PATIENT table and the SURGERY table (the line labeled 1:N is drawn only to assist the reader in visualizing the relationship between the tables).

The SURGERY table contains data about surgeries that patients have undergone. Each recorded surgery is uniquely identified by a SURGERY_ID. The PATIENT table contains data about patients. Each patient is uniquely identified by a PATIENT_ID. The relationship between the SURGERY table and the PATIENT table is based on the identi-

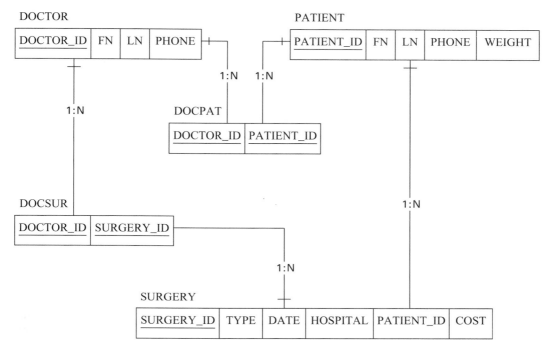

Figure 1.5   Example of Relational Data Model for MEDICAL Database That Accounts for Many-to-Many (N:M) Relationships

fication number of a patient. Cross referencing a PATIENT_ID in the SURGERY table to the corresponding PATIENT_ID in the PATIENT table allows us (or the computer) to associate a patient (by name and phone number) with any surgeries that the patient has undergone. In general, tables are related by placing common columns (which draw their values from the same domain) within multiple tables.

RELATIONAL DATA MANIPULATION

The power of the relational approach is reflected in its data manipulation operators, as was suggested by our discussion on cross referencing a PATIENT_ID in the SURGERY table to a corresponding PATIENT_ID in the PATIENT table. The basic relational operators allow you to retrieve information from a database in a very flexible and powerful way, without requiring you to be familiar with the details of computer programming.

    Three often-used operators are

- SELECT,
- PROJECT, and
- JOIN.

A	B	C	D
a1	b1	c1	d1
a2	b2	c2	d2
a3	b3	c3	d3
a4	b4	c4	d4
a5	b5	c5	d5

SELECT ⟶

A	B	C	D
a2	b2	c2	d2
a3	b3	c3	d3
a4	b4	c4	d4

A	B	C	D
a1	b1	c1	d1
a2	b2	c2	d2
a3	b3	c3	d3
a4	b4	c4	d4
a5	b5	c5	d5

PROJECT

B	C
b1	c1
b2	c2
b3	c3
b4	c4
b5	c5

A	B	C	D
a1	b1	c1	d1
a2	b2	c2	d2
a3	b3	c3	d3
a4	b4	c4	d4
a5	b5	c5	d5

B	E	F	G
b1	e1	f1	g1
b2	e2	f2	g2
b3	e3	f3	g3
b4	e4	f4	g4
b5	e5	f5	g5

JOIN

A	B	C	D	E	F	G
a1	b1	c1	d1	e1	f1	g1
a2	b2	c2	d2	e2	f2	g2
a3	b3	c3	d3	e3	f3	g3
a4	b4	c4	d4	e4	f4	g4
a5	b5	c5	d5	e5	f5	g5

Figure 1.6 Relational Data Manipulation Operators

The SELECT operator supports the extraction of a specified set of rows from a table. The PROJECT operator supports the extraction of a specified set of columns from a table. The JOIN operator results in the rows of one table being concatenated with the rows of another table, based on a specified condition that references similar columns in each table (that is, columns that share the same domain). Figure 1.6 illustrates the operations of the SELECT, PROJECT, and JOIN operators. Please note that the SQL SELECT statement (discussed later in this book) is not the equivalent of the relational operator SELECT. In fact, the SQL SELECT statement will be used to perform relational SELECT, PROJECT, and JOIN operations.

Other relational data manipulation operators include UNION, INTERSECTION, DIFFERENCE, DIVIDE, and PRODUCT. The particulars of these operators are beyond the scope of this book. The interested reader is referred to E. F. Codd's work *The Relational Model for Database Management Version 2* for his definitive discussions of the various relational operators.

KEYS

Keys are identifiers. They direct us to specific data in a table. The three kinds of keys of particular significance in a database are (1) the primary key, (2) the secondary key (alternate key), and (3) the foreign key.

A primary key uniquely identifies a collection of data items. In relational terms, forming a primary key means choosing a column (or aggregate group of columns) with unique values that can be used to identify each row within the table. In Figure 1.2, the SURGERY_ID column is a primary key. Each row has a different surgery identification number. For example, the SURGERY_ID value 3150 appears only once in the entire table and can be used to identify the row containing data on the heart surgery that was performed at Fairfax hospital on 11/30/92 for patient 2000. If values from two or more columns are used to form the key, then the key is referred to as a composite primary key.

Although, strictly speaking, the value within a column (for example, 3150) is the key, not the column itself (for example, SURGERY_ID), in this text we will define and refer to keys by the column names under which the values exist. Thus, we state that the primary key for the SURGERY table is SURGERY_ID. In Figure 1.5 (and in figures throughout this book) primary keys are identified by underlining the column titles that comprise the key.

A secondary key does not uniquely identify a collection of data items. In contrast to a primary key, a secondary key is used to identify a collection of rows that share a particular value in a column (or select group of columns). For example, the column HOSPITAL in Figure 1.2 may be used as a secondary key to identify all of the rows in the SURGERY table that have a value of 'Fairfax' (that is, to identify those rows containing data related to Fairfax hospital). If two or more columns are used to form the key, then the key is referred to as a composite secondary key.

A foreign key is a column that exists in a table for which it is not the primary key, yet also exists as a column in another table for which it is the primary key. For example, in Figure 1.1 (and Figure 1.5) the patient identification number (PATIENT_ID) does not uniquely identify a row (is not a primary key) in the SURGERY table, but it does unique-ly identify a row in the PATIENT table (it is the primary key to PATIENT). A foreign key, like a primary or secondary key, may be formed from a single column or a collection of columns.

VIEWS

In physical reality, the relational database depicted in Figure 1.5 would exist as a collection of data files that paralleled the normalized tables. For example, one file would exist to represent the DOCTOR table, another file would represent the SURGERY table, and so forth.

> **D E F I N I T I O N**
>
> A **physical database** is the collection of actual data files that exist to facilitate the integration and sharing of data across applications and among various users.

Although the database has a single *physical* form, not all users may perceive the same form. For reasons of security or functional segregation, it may be appropriate to limit what users perceive as "the database" to just those items that are relevant to their particular needs.

Views are the means by which this logical dissection of a physical database is accomplished. A view contains no actual data, but instead is a redefinition of another table (or collection of tables). The table that contains the actual data used as the basis of a view is called the base table. Since the view contains no data on its own, it is called a virtual table. Whereas a base table actually exists as a physical database file (takes up space on the computer storage device), a virtual database file exists only in definition (it refers to the data that actually exist in the physical database).

With reference to Figure 1.5, assume that the cost associated with a surgery is restricted information. However, data on the types of surgeries by date and hospital are not restricted—this information can be available to all users. To create a view, we define a table that provides the same data on surgery types and date as the SURGERY table, but excludes the cost data. We don't create another table, but rather define a different way to look at the SURGERY table.

DATABASE INTEGRITY

Maintaining the integrity of the data in a database is crucial to ensuring that the information processed from the database is accurate. As values are added to the database, they should be checked to ensure that they are acceptable in terms of domain and their relationships to other items in the database.

Modifications must be made in a consistent fashion to data stored in the tables that comprise a relational database. For example, in updating tables, care must be exercised to ensure that the data placed in one table do not compromise the data in another table.

Consider the ramifications of deleting a row in the DOCTOR table in the MEDICAL database in Figure 1.5. If you delete a row such as

```
1000     Joe     Smith     555-4444
```

from the DOCTOR table, then you must also delete those rows in the DOCPAT and DOC-SUR tables that include a reference to the DOCTOR_ID (doctor identification number) 1000. Otherwise, the database will have patients under the care of a doctor who does not exist and surgeries taking place without known doctors.

Although the SURGERY table does not contain the DOCTOR_ID field, it too will be affected by the deletion of a row in the DOCTOR table. This is true because entries in the SURGERY table are related to the entries in the DOCSUR table. A row in the SURGERY table that has no corresponding row in the DOCSUR table should be deleted. If not, the surgery will be recorded as taking place without a doctor. This dependency of data contained in one table on the data contained in another table is referred to as referential integrity.

D E F I N I T I O N

Referential integrity is the assurance that values existing in one relation do not exist in the absence of associated values in other relations, as defined by the relational data model.

SUMMARY

Data management has evolved from the limited approach of confining data to a specific computer program to organizing data as separate named collections (data files) to the present-day approach of systematically organizing data in a database.

One method of storing data in a database is the relational approach. In a relational database approach, data are stored as a collection of logically related two-dimensional tables that abide by certain rules. The normalization process is used to build a collection of tables in an acceptable form. The normalization process classifies the analysis of data items into tables of first normal form (1NF), second normal form (2NF), third normal form (3NF), Boyce/Codd normal form (BCNF), fourth normal form (4NF), and fifth normal form (5NF).

In deriving tables that are normalized, the relational database approach is to determine how the various tables are related to one another. Three types of relationships may exist: one to one, one to many, and many to many. The relationships that exist in a relational database are carried within the data. There are no separate structures used to represent how one data item refers to another.

The power of the relational approach is reflected in its data manipulation operators. Three often-used operators are SELECT, PROJECT, and JOIN.

Other topics discussed in this first chapter included keys, views, and database integrity. Keys are identifiers. Three kinds of keys are of particular significance in a database: primary keys, secondary keys, and foreign keys. Although the database has a single physical form, not all users may perceive the same form. A view is a logical dissection of a physical database—a view contains no actual data, but instead is a redefinition of another table (or collection of tables). Maintaining the integrity of the data in a database is crucial to ensuring that the information processed from the database is accurate.

ENDNOTES

1. James Martin, *Managing the Data-Base Environment* (Englewood Cliffs, N.J.: Prentice-Hall, 1983), p. 4.
2. E. F. Codd, "A Relational Model of Data for Large Shared Data Banks," *Communications of the ACM*, vol. 13, No. 6 (June 1970): pp. 377–387.
3. E. F. Codd, *The Relational Model for Database Management Version 2* (pp. 15–16), copyright 1990 by Addison-Wesley Publishing Company, Inc. Reprinted by permission.
4. C. J. Date, *An Introduction to Database Systems*, 5th ed., volume 1, copyright 1990 by Addison-Wesley Publishing Company, Inc. Reprinted by permission.
5. E. F. Codd, "A Relational Model of Data for Large Shared Data Banks," p. 381.

QUESTIONS

1. What is a database?
2. How do the relational terms *relation*, *attribute*, *tuple*, and *domain* compare with the common terms for a table of information?
3. What is normalization and what is its role?
4. What does it mean to advance a table from 1NF to 2NF?
5. In Figure 1.4, what is the relationship between the DOCTOR table and the SURGERY table? Discuss what the relationship implies.
6. What are the relational operators? Discuss their relevance and use.
7. What types of keys may exist in a database?
8. What is a foreign key? Give an example.
9. What is a view? How are views different from other relational forms?
10. What is referential integrity?

EXERCISES

1. Draw a diagram, similar to Figure 1.4, that depicts the relationships between an entity on students (STUDENTS), an entity on the courses that students have attended (COURSES), and an entity about those who taught the courses (TEACHERS).

2. Adjust the data model in Figure 1.5 to include data on the addresses (with zip codes) of surgeons and patients.

2

Defining SQL

DATABASE LANGUAGES

A major objective in moving to a database environment is to better meet the information processing needs of an organization. These needs are serviced through applications.

> **DEFINITION**
>
> An **application** is a request made of the database. An application is typified by a block of code that performs a function.

An application may call for information to be displayed on the screen, or it may require that a report be generated (on, for example, the surgeries a patient has undergone).

The speed, flexibility, and cost-effectiveness of database application development are determined mainly by the languages that are supported by the database management system (DBMS). A DBMS is a set of computer programs that are used to define, process, and administer the database and its applications.[1] There are three broad categories into which DBMS languages may be classified. The categories are

1. data definition language (DDL),
2. data manipulation language (DML), and
3. query language.

A DDL is used to build the data structures that define the database. A DML provides for data control and allows high-level programming languages such as COBOL or the C language to interface with the database. A query language is an end-user language; that is, non-technical people can use it to retrieve information from the database without mastering computer programming skills.

Although the AS/400 offers alternative ways to create files (such as a database structure) and a clever programmer may find ways to use COBOL or the C language to create and manipulate database files, the AS/400 implementation of SQL effectively provides a DDL, a DML, and a query language.

THE ESSENCE OF SQL

The AS/400 implementation of SQL serves as an application development tool that may be used for data definition, data control and manipulation, and query.

SQL stands for structured query language. It is an English keyword–oriented language that is used to store and manipulate data in a relational database. SQL was first developed at IBM under the name SEQUEL during the mid 1970s. Today SQL has become an American National Standards Institute (ANSI) standard and the de facto industry standard for relational database languages.

In an age when the computing needs of many organizations require the transfer of data among multiple information systems operating on all types of computers, a common database language is necessary. SQL is not only a powerful integration tool, but also a language that is easily learned by all users.

SQL is not a programming language like COBOL, RPG, or the C language. It does not require you to code an elaborate collection of procedural statements to accomplish a task (for example, a sequence of instructions to open a file, read a record, process the record, read another record, and so forth). An SQL statement only a few lines long can yield a report that would have required pages of program code in a language such as COBOL. In addition, an SQL statement may be processed as it is entered, providing an immediate response to a database query.

> ### D E F I N I T I O N
> A **query** is an interactive request for information that is made of the database. When you query the database using SQL, the specified tables are processed and the resulting information is provided (usually displayed on the screen) in the form of a two-dimensional table.

Perhaps the greatest benefit in adopting the database approach and the use of SQL is that users (both technical and non-technical) can quickly and easily retrieve information, including data that otherwise could not be retrieved (at least not without expensive, time-consuming programming). By using Interactive SQL to query the database, a user can obtain information immediately!

SQL can be either embedded or interactive. Although a brief explanation of embedded SQL follows, the focus of this text will be on Interactive SQL.

Embedded SQL on the AS/400

Although SQL is not like COBOL, RPG, or the C programming language, SQL statements may be embedded within a program coded in these (or other) high-level languages supported on the AS/400. High-level languages provide mechanisms for repetitive execution of statements (looping) and extensive report formatting; SQL does not. By using embedded SQL (also referred to at static SQL), the programmer can retain the procedural power of a high-level language while taking advantage of the data manipulation power of SQL.

When SQL is coded within a high-level language, the latter is referred to as the host language. The program coded using SQL statements and host language statements is first processed by a pre-compiler. The pre-compiler replaces the SQL statements with statements that are a part of the host language. The adjusted program is then compiled, linked, and executed as though it contained no SQL. The Programming option on the AS/400's main menu leads to a submenu (whose system menu name is PROGRAM) that includes the Structured Query Language (SQL) Pre compiler option, which provides an appropriate tool for working with embedded SQL.

Interactive SQL on the AS/400

To query a database with Interactive SQL on the AS/400, the user enters statements at a computer terminal.* The statements are processed as they are entered, and the information requested, or an error message, is displayed immediately after each statement is processed. Status messages may also be displayed if a statement takes an unusually long time to execute.

There are four basic functions that are a part of the AS/400 Interactive SQL language:[2]

1. Statement entry: SQL statements are simply typed in at the keyboard and processed.
2. Prompt function: This function provides guidance on the proper syntax/options of a statement. The user enters part of a statement (e.g., CREATE) and then presses function key four (F4) to receive help.
3. Session services: Various services are available, such as changing the list of collections and changing the output device.
4. List selection: Authorized collections, tables, views, or columns can be selected and inserted at the cursor position.

These four basic functions form a powerful interactive language that may be used to create, maintain, and query a relational database. These functions enhance the productivity of SQL users and can have a significant impact on the amount of time and effort it takes to manage information.

*Chapter 3 introduces the AS/400 commands and menus that are pertinent to the use of Interactive SQL on the AS/400. For general information on the AS/400 computer and its use, refer to Appendixes B and C.

SQL Limits on the AS/400

Although SQL offers the non-technical user a relatively simple means to store and process data in a database, it is limited. As noted earlier, SQL does not provide for repetitive execution of statements (looping) or extensive report formatting. SQL also does not offer much in the way of data validation. High-level languages such as COBOL or the C language must fill these voids.

SQL as practiced on the AS/400 also has certain limits. Table 2.1 details some of the more important SQL limits, such as minimum and maximum values that are imposed by the AS/400 system. These limits are important to note because they define the boundaries within which work with SQL on the AS/400 must fall. In addition, only a limited number of SQL statements are available for interactive processing. Table 2.2 summarizes the SQL statements that are available for interactive processing on the AS/400.

TABLE 2.1 AS/400 SQL LIMITS

Component	AS/400 SQL Limit
Longest SQL identifier	10
Most columns in a table	8,000
Most columns in a view	8,000
Maximum length of a row (in bytes)	32,766
Maximum byte count of CHAR	32,766
Largest INTEGER value	− 2,147,483,647
Smallest INTEGER value	2,147,483,648
Largest SMALLINT value	− 32,767
Smallest SMALLINT value	32,768
Largest FLOAT value	Approx. 1.79E308
Smallest FLOAT value	Approx. −1.79E308
Largest REAL value	Approx. 3.40E38
Smallest REAL value	Approx. −3.40E38
Longest SQL statement	32,767 bytes
Most elements in a select list	8,000 or less
Most predicates in a WHERE clause	4,690
Maximum number of columns in a GROUP BY clause	120
Maximum number of columns in an ORDER BY clause	10,000
Most columns in an index key	120
Longest index key	2,000

Source: Application System/400: Systems Application Architecture Structured Query Language/400 Reference (SC41-9608-03), Version 2, IBM Corporation, 4th ed. (November 1993), pp. 283–285.

TABLE 2.2 AVAILABLE AS/400 INTERACTIVE SQL STATEMENTS

COMMENT ON	Replaces or adds a comment to the description of a table, view, column, or package.
COMMIT	Terminates a unit of recovery and commits the database changes made by that unit of recovery.
CREATE COLLECTION	Defines a collection.
CREATE INDEX	Defines an index on a table.
CREATE TABLE	Defines a table.
CREATE VIEW	Defines a view.
DELETE	Deletes one or more rows from a table.
DROP	Deletes a collection, table, index, view, or package.
GRANT	Grants privileges on a table, view, or package.
INSERT	Inserts data into a table.
LABEL ON	Replaces or adds a label on the description of a table, view, column, or package.
LOCK TABLE	Locks a table in shared or exclusive mode.
REVOKE	Revokes privileges on a table, view, or package.
ROLLBACK	Terminates a unit of recovery and backs out the database changes made by that unit of recovery.
SELECT	Specifies a query action.
UPDATE	Updates the values of one or more columns in one or more rows of a table.

Source: Application System/400: Systems Application Architecture Structured Query Language/400 Programmer's Guide (SC41-9609-03), Version 2, IBM Corporation, 4th ed. (November 1993), p. 10-2.

AS/400 Terminology

Recall from our discussion in Chapter 1 that a *database* is a collection of interrelated data stored together to facilitate the integration and sharing of data across applications and among various users. In a *relational database,* data storage and management is accomplished by defining a collection of tables that are related through the existence of common columns within the various tables.

Special terminology is used by SQL, the AS/400 operating system, and the AS/400's data storage. For example, the relational data model depicted in Figure 2.1 would be implemented as a single database, perhaps called the MEDICAL database. In AS/400 SQL terminology, a database is referred to as a *collection*. On the AS/400, when a table is created it is assigned to exactly one collection. The rows in a table are akin to records. The columns are akin to fields.

Anything that takes up storage space on the AS/400 is called an object (see Appendix B for more information). A collection (otherwise known as a database) is one type of object on the AS/400 operating system. In AS/400 data storage terms, a collection is called a library. In storage terms, a table will be stored on the AS/400 as a physical file and placed as an object into the named library (collection). In data storage terms, the MEDICAL database illustrated in Figure 2.1 would physically exist on the AS/400 within a user-defined library. Thus, a user library contains both user-defined data and objects, and one kind of object is the database file.

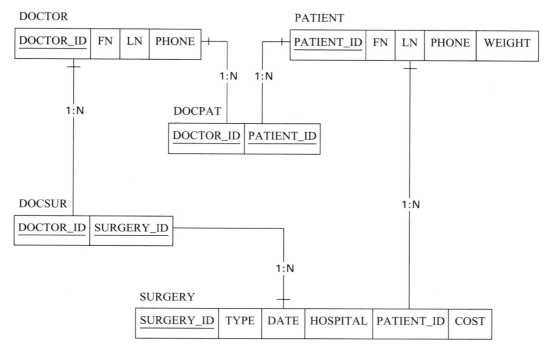

Figure 2.1 Example of Relational MEDICAL Database

A database file may exist as a physical file or as a logical file. A physical file contains actual application data, whereas a logical file is simply a redefinition of a physical file. Logical files allow for different views of the same physical file (see the discussion on views in Chapter 1).

AS/400 SQL terms and the corresponding AS/400 data storage terms are summarized in Table 2.3. See Appendix B for more information on data storage on the AS/400.

TABLE 2.3 AS/400 SQL TERMS AND
CORRESPONDING STORAGE TERMS

AS/400 SQL Term	AS/400 Data Storage Term
Collection	Library
Table	Physical file
Row	Record
Column	Field
View	Logical file

Source: Application System/400: Systems Application Architecture Structured Query Language/400 Programmer's Guide (SC41-9609-03), Version 2, IBM Corporation, 4th ed. (November 1993), pp. 1-3 and 12-1.

ELEMENTS OF AN SQL STATEMENT

The AS/400 Interactive SQL statements fall into two broad categories: data definition and data manipulation. The data definition statements include CREATE COLLECTION, CREATE INDEX, CREATE TABLE, CREATE VIEW, COMMENT ON, LABEL ON, DROP, GRANT, and REVOKE. The data manipulation statements include COMMIT, INSERT, LOCK TABLE, ROLLBACK, DELETE, SELECT, and UPDATE.

Although each Interactive SQL statement has its own particular syntax, all are made up of the same basic components and share the same language elements. Language elements include statement verbs; naming of tables, columns, or views; keywords; expressions; and search conditions. Consider the following satement, which queries the MEDICAL database for information on patients who have undergone heart surgery:

```
SELECT SURGERY.PATIENT_ID, SURGERY.TYPE, SURGERY.HOSPITAL
   FROM MEDICAL/SURGERY
   WHERE TYPE = 'Heart'
```

The verb SELECT requests that the SURGERY table be searched and that a table of information (composed of the columns PATIENT_ID, TYPE, and HOSPITAL) be provided based on the result of the search. The table produced is referred to as the *resulting table*. As the components of this statement are typical of the many Interactive SQL statements you will enter, let's examine it in more detail.

Our example qualified each column name using the naming convention

```
table-name.column-name
```

The period (.) separates the name of the table from the column name. Since the same column name may exist in other tables within the same collection, this naming convention allows us to specify precisely which column to use. This naming convention is crucial when our statements reference multiple tables. In our example only one table is referenced, so we could eliminate the table name and period, implicitly naming the columns.

Following the keyword FROM we specify the table in which the named columns exist. Our example qualified the table name using the naming convention

```
collection-name/table-name
```

The slash (/) separates the name of the collection (database) from the table name. Since the same table name may exist in other collections, this naming convention allows us to specify which collection to use. The slash (/) is the AS/400 system default. As is discussed later in this book, you may change this to the period (.), as is used in many other implementations of SQL.

Another important part of our example SELECT statement is the specification of search criteria. The WHERE clause is often used in an SQL statement to specify particular rows of a table for consideration. The expression TYPE = 'Heart' restricts the extraction of rows to only those with the value 'Heart' in their TYPE of surgery column. The equal to (=) operator is one of several that are available and will be discussed later in this book.

Although each Interactive SQL statement will have its own syntax, these basic elements—the WHERE clause to restrict a statement to certain rows and the period (.) or the slash (/) to qualify the names of columns or tables—will appear in other statements.

SUMMARY

A database environment improves the speed, flexibility, and cost-effectiveness of the development of applications to meet the information processing needs of an organization. The database management system (DBMS) includes a data definition language (DDL), a data manipulation language (DML), and a query language. The AS/400 implementation of SQL effectively provides all three elements of a database management system.

SQL stands for structured query language. It is an ANSI standard language that is used to store and manipulate data in a relational database. SQL is both a powerful integration tool and a language that can be mastered quickly by the non-technical user.

SQL comes in two forms: embedded and interactive. Embedded SQL allows the programmer to retain the procedural power of a high-level language while taking advantage of the data manipulation power of SQL. Interactive SQL is a powerful query language that can be used to query a database for immediate responses. Commands are processed as they are entered at a computer terminal, and the information requested or an error message is displayed immediately.

To effectively employ SQL on the AS/400 requires an understanding of the relational database approach to organizing and manipulating data. The relational database approach is based on the concept of storing data as a series of logically related two-dimensional tables. The AS/400 uses its own terminology for the relational approach. In AS/400, the overall collection of related tables is called a collection rather than a database. The AS/400 also has data storage terms. For example, a collection is akin to a library. On the AS/400, when a table (a physical file) is created, it is assigned to exactly one collection (a library).

The available AS/400 Interactive SQL statements fall into two broad categories: data definition and data manipulation. The data definition statements include CREATE COLLECTION, CREATE INDEX, CREATE TABLE, CREATE VIEW, COMMENT ON, LABEL ON, DROP, GRANT, and REVOKE. The data manipulation statements include COMMIT, INSERT, LOCK TABLE, ROLLBACK, DELETE, SELECT, and UPDATE. Although each Interactive SQL statement has its own particular syntax, all are made up of the same basic components and share the same language elements.

ENDNOTES

1. David M. Kroenke, *Database Processing: Fundamentals, Design, Implementation*, 4th ed. (New York: Macmillan, 1992), p. 52.

2. *Application System/400: Systems Application Architecture Structured Query Language/400 Programmer's Guide (SC41-9609-03)*, *Version 2*, IBM Corporation, 4th ed. (November 1993), pp. 12-1 and 12-2.

QUESTIONS

1. What is an application? What is the role of applications in a database environment?
2. What are the three major categories of database languages?
3. For what purpose might a DDL be used?
4. For what purpose might a DML be used?
5. How does SQL differ from a high-level language like COBOL?
6. What is a host language?
7. What is the difference between Interactive SQL and embedded SQL?
8. What are the limits of Interactive SQL on the AS/400?
9. How do the AS/400 data storage terms *library*, *physical file*, *record*, and *field* relate to SQL?
10. What are the major elements of an Interactive SQL statement?

EXERCISES

1. Code a COBOL or C program that accomplishes the same reporting function as our example SQL statement:

   ```
   SELECT SURGERY.PATIENT_ID, SURGERY.TYPE, SURGERY.HOSPITAL
      FROM MEDICAL/SURGERY
      WHERE TYPE = 'Heart'
   ```

2. Discuss the four basic functions that are a part of the AS/400 Interactive SQL language, and contrast their services with those provided with programming support environments currently available for high-level languages such as BASIC and C.

3

Entering/Exiting
Interactive SQL

THE SIGN-ON PROCESS

Starting a work session on the AS/400 requires establishing communication between your work station and the AS/400. This process, referred to as the sign-on process, will vary from

```
    MAIN                          AS/400 MAIN MENU
                                                      SYSTEM: NVAS400
    SELECT ONE OF THE FOLLOWING:

         1. USER TASKS
         2. OFFICE TASKS
         3. GENERAL SYSTEM TASKS
         4. FILES, LIBRARIES, AND FOLDERS
         5. PROGRAMMING
         6. COMMUNICATIONS
         7. DEFINE OR CHANGE THE SYSTEM
         8. PROBLEM HANDLING
         9. DISPLAY A MENU
        10. INFORMATION ASSISTANT OPTIONS

        90. SIGN OFF

    SELECTION OR COMMAND
    ===>_

    F3=EXIT F4=PROMPT F9=RETRIEVE F12=CANCEL F13=INFO ASSISTANT
    F23=SET INITIAL MENU
                            © COPYRIGHT IBM CORP. 1980, 1993
```

Figure 3.1   The AS/400 MAIN MENU Screen

Note: Copyrighted screens in this chapter are used by permission of IBM Corporation.

one site to another. At some installations, you must request access to the AS/400 from a selection of available systems. Appendix B describes one such process. Consult your system administrator or instructor to learn how to gain access to your AS/400 computer.

The AS/400 MAIN MENU screen is the first one presented following entry into the AS/400 system (see Figure 3.1). To select an option from the MAIN MENU, simply enter the corresponding number of the desired option at the command prompt

```
SELECTION OR COMMAND
===>_
```

and then press the Enter key. Appendixes B and C contain additional information on the general access and use of the AS/400.

HOW TO START AN INTERACTIVE SQL SESSION

After signing on to the AS/400 system, you may start an Interactive SQL session by

1. choosing it as an option from the DECISION SUPPORT menu (see the following section)

   or

2. entering the control language (CL) command STRSQL at the command prompt that is presented at the bottom of any AS/400 menu screen.

D E F I N I T I O N

The phrase **enter a command** means to type the desired command and then press the Enter key. Please note that the Enter key and the Return key do not have the same effect, unlike these keys on a personal computer. The Enter key signals the system to process what has been typed. The Return key (often symbolized by an arrow bent to the left) simply moves the cursor down a line. The Backspace key or arrow keys may be used to correct a typing error prior to pressing the Enter key.

Traversing Menus to Enter Interactive SQL

There are two ways to reach the DECISION SUPPORT menu, where Interactive SQL is an option. The first is to traverse through the menus. From the MAIN MENU, depicted in Figure 3.1, choose the second option (OFFICE TASKS) by entering a "2" at the command prompt. The system responds with the OFFICE TASKS menu depicted in Figure 3.2.

From the OFFICE TASKS menu, choose the third option (DECISION SUPPORT) by entering a "3" at the command prompt. The system responds with the DECISION SUPPORT menu depicted in Figure 3.3.

From the DECISION SUPPORT menu, choose the fourth option (INTERACTIVE SQL) by entering a "4" at the command prompt. The system responds with the Interactive SQL screen depicted in Figure 3.4. Interactive SQL statements can then be entered.

```
OFCTSK                          OFFICE TASKS
                                              SYSTEM: NVAS400
SELECT ONE OF THE FOLLOWING:

     1. AS/400 OFFICE - OFFICEVISION/400
     2. HOST SYSTEM TASKS FOR AS/400 PC SUPPORT
     3. DECISION SUPPORT
     4. OFFICE SECURITY
     5. DISPLAY SYSTEM DIRECTORY
     6. WORK WITH SYSTEM DIRECTORY
     7. DOCUMENTS
     8. FOLDERS

    70. RELATED COMMANDS



SELECTION OR COMMAND
===>_

F3=EXIT F4=PROMPT F9=RETRIEVE F12=CANCEL F13=INFO ASSISTANT
F16=SYSTEM MAIN MENU
                          © COPYRIGHT IBM CORP. 1980, 1993
```

Figure 3.2   The AS/400 OFFICE TASKS Menu Screen

```
DECISION                    DECISION SUPPORT
                                              SYSTEM: NVAS400
SELECT ONE OF THE FOLLOWING:

     1. INTERACTIVE DATA DEFINITION UTILITY (IDDU)
     2. QUERY
     3. BUSINESS GRAPHICS UTILITY (BGU)
     4. INTERACTIVE SQL


    20. FILES


    70. RELATED COMMANDS



SELECTION OR COMMAND
===>_

F3=EXIT F4=PROMPT F9=RETRIEVE F12=CANCEL F13=INFO ASSISTANT
F16=SYSTEM MAIN MENU
                          © COPYRIGHT IBM CORP. 1980, 1993
```

Figure 3.3   The AS/400 DECISION SUPPORT Menu Screen

```
┌──────────────────────────────────────────────────────────────────────┐
│                       ENTER SQL STATEMENTS                             │
│                                                                        │
│    TYPE SQL STATEMENT, PRESS ENTER                                     │
│                                                                        │
│    ===>_                                                               │
│                                                                        │
│                                                                        │
│                                                                        │
│                                                                        │
│                                                                        │
│                                                                        │
│                                                                        │
│                                                                        │
│                                                                        │
│                                                                        │
│    F3=EXIT F4=PROMPT F6=INSERT LINE F9=RETRIEVE F10=COPY LINE          │
│    F12=CANCEL          F13=SERVICES    F24=MORE KEYS                    │
└──────────────────────────────────────────────────────────────────────┘
```

Figure 3.4   The Interactive SQL Screen

Menu Shortcut

A second way to traverse menus is to use the GO command. Entering the GO command along with the name of the desired menu causes the system to jump directly to that menu. Thus, if you enter

                              ===>GO DECISION

at the command prompt, the system jumps directly to the DECISION SUPPORT menu. You can then choose the INTERACTIVE SQL option by entering a "4" at the command prompt. The system responds with the Interactive SQL screen depicted in Figure 3.4. Interactive SQL statements can then be entered.

The STRSQL Command

The fastest way to start an Interactive SQL session is to enter the STRSQL command at the command prompt

                              ===>STRSQL

The system responds directly with the Interactive SQL screen depicted in Figure 3.4. Interactive SQL statements can then be entered.

BOO BOO BOX	`COMMAND STARTSQL IN LIBRARY *LIBL NOT FOUND.` If you misspell the STRSQL command, you will receive an error message similar to the one above. In this case the command was erroneously spelled STARTSQL. No harm is done. To correct the error, simply type the command correctly (at the command prompt) and press the Enter key.

INTERACTIVE SQL FUNCTION KEYS

Note that the list of defined function keys on the bottom of the Interactive SQL screen depicted in Figure 3.4 differs from the list displayed on the AS/400 menu screens. The displayed function keys now include F3, F4, F6, F9, F10, F12, F13, and F24. If you press F24 (MORE KEYS), your selection of function keys will change to include F14, F15, F16, F17, F18, and F24. The definitions of these function keys, as well as some others that are not listed on the screen but nonetheless are available for your use, follow:

F1=HELP	Provides information on using the system. The information displayed depends on where you are when you request help. Help is context sensitive, which means the information provided is relative to the ongoing action.
F3=EXIT	Ends the current Interactive SQL session (see the discussion on how to end an Interactive SQL session), returning you to the AS/400 menu screen from which you started the session.
F4=PROMPT	Provides assistance in entering or selecting a statement.
F6=INSERT LINE	Inserts a blank line below the line where the cursor is located.
F7=SCROLL BACKWARD	When working with multiple screens of information, you will see the note "MORE..." on the bottom right side of the screen. As you read through the multiple screens, you may use this function key to return you to the previous screen.
F8=SCROLL FORWARD	When working with multiple screens of information, you will see the note "MORE..." on the bottom right side of the screen. You use this function key to advance to the next screen of information.

F9=RETRIEVE

Retrieves a previously entered SQL statement. You may retrieve a previously executed statement by placing the cursor under any part of the statement that is still visible on the screen and then pressing this function key. If the cursor is not under a previously executed statement, then the last statement executed is retrieved.

F10=COPY LINE

Copies all of the line on which the cursor is located to a new line immediately below the line being copied.

F12=CANCEL

Cancels the current display or statement and returns to the previous display.

F13=SERVICES

Displays the SESSION SERVICES menu.

F14=DELETE LINE

Deletes the entire line on which the cursor is located.

F15=SPLIT LINE

Causes everything to the right of the cursor (including the character above the cursor) to be left-justified on a new line immediately below the line where the cursor is located.

F16=SELECT LIBRARIES

Displays a list of available collections or libraries, allowing you to change the name of the currently selected collection or library.

F17=SELECT FILES

Displays a list of available tables (physical files) and views (logical files), based on previously selected collections (libraries).

F18=SELECT FIELDS

Displays a list of available columns (fields), based on previously selected tables or views (files).

F24=MORE KEYS

Causes alternate function keys to be displayed.

A Note on Keyboard Mapping: Depending on the terminal or work station used to access the AS/400, different keystrokes may be required to achieve the same system response. For example, accomplishing the task of "pressing function key one" may mean simply pressing the key labeled F1 or, as is the case with the TELEX 178 Display Terminals, holding down the Alternate (ALT) key and then pressing the 1 key. Consult your system administrator, instructor, or lab assistant for specific instructions.

MORE ON THE STRSQL COMMAND

Although you may enter the STRSQL command by itself, the command offers more. As illustrated by the STRSQL syntax chart in Figure 3.5, the STRSQL command has a number of parameters available that allow you to specify particular processing options. The parameters of the STRSQL command include COMMIT, NAMING, PROCESS, LIBOPT, LISTTYPE, REFRESH, ALWCPYDTA, DATFMT, DATSEP, TIMFMT, TIMSEP, DECPNT, PGMLNG, SQLSTRDLM, SRTSEQ, and LANGID.[1]

```
          ┌──────────────┌─────────┐──────────────────────┌──────┐────────────────────┐
          │      COMMIT ( │ *NONE │ ) NAMING (│ *SYS │) PROCESS ( │ *RUN │ )            │
          │               │ *CHG  │           │ *SQL │            │ *VLD │             │
          │               │ *CS   │                                │ *SYN │           │
          │               │ *ALL  │                                                    │
          │                                                                            │
          │                      │ *LIBL    │                                          │
          │                      │ *CURLIB  │                                          │
          │      LIBOPT (        │ *USRLIBL │ ) LISTTYPE (│ *ALL │)                     │
          │                      │ *ALL     │             │ *SQL │                     │
          │                      │ *ALLUSR  │                                          │
          │                      │ lib name │                                          │
          │                                              *YES                          │
          │      REFRESH (│ *ALWAYS  │) ALWCPYDTA (│ *OPTIMIZE │)                       │
          │               │ *FORWARD │              *NO                                │
          │                                                                            │
          │              │ *JOB │              │ *JOB   │            │ *HMS │          │
          │              │ *USA │              │ *BLANK │            │ *USA │          │
          │              │ *ISO │              │ '/'    │            │ *ISO │          │
STRSQL    │      DATFMT (│ *EUR │) DATSEP (     │ '.'    │ ) TIMFMT (│ *EUR │)         │
          │              │ *JIS │              │ ','    │            │ *JIS │          │
          │              │ *MDY │              │ '-'    │                              │
          │              │ *DMY │              │ ' '    │                              │
          │              │ *YMD │                                                      │
          │              │ *JUL │                                                      │
          │                                                        │ *NONE │          │
          │              │ *JOB   │                                 │ *C    │          │
          │              │ *BLANK │              │ *SYSVAL │        │ *CBL  │          │
          │      TIMSEP (│ ':'    │) DECPNT (    │ *PERIOD │)PGMLNG (│ *PLI │ )        │
          │              │ '.'    │              │ *COMMA  │        │ *RPG  │          │
          │              │ ','    │                                 │ *FTN  │          │
          │              │ ' '    │                                                    │
          │                                                      │ *JOB              │ │
          │                                                      │ *JOBRUN           │ │
          │                                                      │ *LANGIDINQ        │ │
          │      SQLSTRDLM (│ *QUOTESQL │ ) SRTSEQ (  │ *LANGIDSHR          │ )       │
          │                 │ *APOSTSQL │             │ *HEX                │         │
          │                                           │ *LIBL/table-name    │         │
          │                                           │ *CURLIB/table-name  │         │
          │                                           │ *library/table-name │         │
          │              │ *JOB        │                                              │
          │      LANGID (│ *JOBRUN     │)                                             │
          │              │ language-ID │                                              │
          └────────────────────────────────────────────────────────────────────────────┘
```

Figure 3.5   Syntax Chart for STRSQL Command

Note: Parameters that are underlined are the system defaults. Asterisks are part of the IBM syntax and are required. Lowercase names represent variables.

The COMMIT parameter affects the commitment of changes made to a database. More than one user may reference the data in a database at the same time. Locking out another user from referencing your work before you are ready to commit it to the database helps to maintain the integrity of the data in the database. The COMMIT statement applies your changes to the database. In entering the STRSQL command with the COMMIT parameter, you may select

*NONE	Indicates that commitment control is not used. COMMIT and ROLLBACK commands are not allowed.
*CHG	Indicates that only those rows you update, delete, or insert are locked until you COMMIT your work.
*CS	Indicates that all rows you select are locked and then unlocked as they are read. Rows you update, delete, or insert are locked until you COMMIT your work.
*ALL	Indicates that all the rows you select, update, delete, or insert are locked until you COMMIT (or ROLLBACK) your work.

The NAMING parameter is used to specify which naming convention will be used in naming objects such as tables or columns in your SQL statements. You may select

*SYS	Indicates that the AS/400 system naming convention will be used — that is, a slash ('/') separates the library name from the file name (for example, MEDICAL/PATIENT).
*SQL	Indicates that the SQL naming convention will be used—that is, a period ('.') separates the library name from the file name (for example, MEDICAL.PATIENT).

The PROCESS parameter is used to specify whether your statements should actually process data values. You may select

*RUN	Indicates that the SQL statements you enter are to be syntax checked, data checked, and then executed.
*VLD	Indicates that the SQL statements you enter are to be syntax checked and data checked, but not executed.
*SYN	Indicates that the SQL statements you enter are to be syntax checked only.

The LIBOPT parameter is used to specify which collections or libraries are to be used as a basis for building a list when any of the function keys F16, F17, F18, or F4 is pressed. You may select

*LIBL	Indicates that all the libraries in the user and system portions of the job's library list should be displayed.

*CURLIB — Indicates that the current library should be displayed.

*USRLIBL — Indicates that only the libraries in the user portion of the job's library list should be displayed.

*ALL — Indicates that all the libraries in the system, including QSYS, should be displayed.

*ALLUSR — Indicates that all the non-system libraries, which include the QGPL library and all user-defined libraries that are not in the job's library list, are to be displayed. Libraries whose names start with the letter Q, other than QGPL, are not included.

Library-name — Permits you to specify the name of a library. (You enter the name of the particular library you want.)

The LISTTYPE parameter is used to specify what types of objects are to be displayed with list support (F16, F17, F18, or F4). You may select

*ALL — Indicates that all objects are to be displayed.

*SQL — Indicates that only objects created with SQL are to be displayed.

The REFRESH parameter is used to indicate when the data that are displayed as a result of a SELECT statement should be refreshed (revised to show any changes that others may have made since the statement was executed). You may select

*ALWAYS — Indicates that the data should be refreshed as you page forward and backward through the screens of data displayed.

*FORWARD — Indicates that the data should be refreshed only as you page forward to the end of the data for the first time. When you page backward, a copy of the data you have already seen is displayed.

The ALWCPYDTA parameter is used to specify whether a copy of the data is to be used in a SELECT statement. If COMMIT (*ALL) is specified, then the ALWCPYDTA value is ignored and the system uses the actual data. You may select

*YES — A copy of the data is allowed.

*OPTIMIZE — The system determines, based on performance, whether to use the data retrieved or a copy.

*NO — A copy of the data is not allowed.

The DATFMT parameter indicates the date format used in SQL statements. You may select

*JOB — The format specified by the job attribute DATFMT is used.

*USA — The United States date format of mm/dd/yyyy is used.

*ISO	The International Standards Organization date format of yyyy-mm-dd is used.
*EUR	The European date format of dd.mm.yyyy is used.
*JIS	The Japanese Industry Standard Christian Era date format of yyyy-mm-dd is used.
*MDY	The format of mm/dd/yy is used.
*DMY	The format of dd/mm/yy is used.
*YMD	The format of yy/mm/dd is used.
*JUL	The Julian date format of yy/ddd is used.

The DATSEP parameter indicates the date separator used in SQL statements. You may select

*JOB	The date separator specified on the job attribute is used.
*BLANK	A blank is used.
'/'	A slash is used.
'.'	A period is used.
','	A comma is used.
'-'	A dash (or minus sign) is used.
' '	A blank is used.

The TIMFMT parameter indicates the time format used in SQL statements. You may select

*HMS	The format of hour-minute-second (hh:mm:ss) is used.
*USA	The United States format of hh:mm.ss is used.
*ISO	The International Standards Organization format of hh.mm.ss is used.
*EUR	The European format of hh.mm.ss is used.
*JIS	The Japanese Industry Standard Christian Era format of hh:mm:ss is used.

The TIMSEP parameter indicates the time separator used in SQL statements. You may select.

*JOB	The time separator specified on the job attribute is used.
*BLANK	A blank is used.
':'	A colon is used.
'.'	A period is used.
','	A comma is used.
' '	A blank is used.

The DECPNT parameter is used to specify what kind of decimal point you want to use. You may select

*SYSVAL	Indicates that the decimal point is to be extracted from the system-defined value.
*PERIOD	Indicates that a period is to represent the decimal point.
*COMMA	Indicates that a comma is to represent the decimal point.

The PGMLNG parameter is used to specify the program language syntax rules to use. To use this parameter, you must have selected *SYN with the PROCESS parameter. You may select

*NONE	Indicates that you are not using any particular language's syntax rules.
*C	The C programming language
*CBL	The COBOL programming language
*PLI	The PL/I programming language
*RPG	The RPG programming language
*FTN	The FORTRAN programming language

The SQLSTRDLM parameter is used to specify the SQL string delimiter. To use this parameter, you must have identified COBOL (*CBL) as your language with the PGMLNG parameter. You may select

*QUOTESQL	Indicates that a quotation mark is to represent the SQL string delimiter.
*APOSTSQL	Indicates that an apostrophe is to represent the SQL string delimiter.

The SRTSEQ parameter indicates the sort sequence table to be used for string comparisons in SQL statements. The LANGID parameter specifies the language identifier to be used when SRTSEQ (*LANGIDUNQ) or SRTSEQ (*LANGIDSHR) is specified.

Example

The command

```
===>STRSQL NAMING(*SQL)
```

starts an Interactive SQL session in which the SQL naming convention (in contrast to the default AS/400 naming convention) must be employed. That is, a period ('.') will be used to separate the library name from the file name (for example, MEDICAL.PATIENT). The AS/400 default (*SYS) would have required that a slash ('/') be used (for example, MED-ICAL/PATIENT).

HOW TO END AN INTERACTIVE SQL SESSION

To terminate an Interactive SQL session and return to the menu system of the AS/400 (from which you may log off the AS/400 system), simply press function key three (F3), as noted on the bottom of the screen (F3=EXIT). After you press F3, the system responds with the Exit Interactive SQL screen depicted in Figure 3.6.

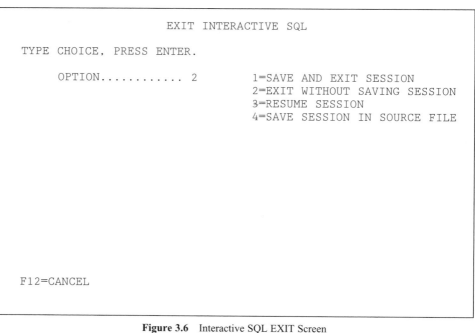

```
                        EXIT INTERACTIVE SQL

   TYPE CHOICE, PRESS ENTER.

           OPTION........... 2         1=SAVE AND EXIT SESSION
                                       2=EXIT WITHOUT SAVING SESSION
                                       3=RESUME SESSION
                                       4=SAVE SESSION IN SOURCE FILE




   F12=CANCEL
```

Figure 3.6   Interactive SQL EXIT Screen

Four options are presented. Choose one of the four options by typing the number of the option and then pressing the Enter key. For example, to exit without saving the session, enter a "2."

The four options on the exit screen are

1=SAVE AND EXIT SESSION	Terminates the Interactive SQL session while saving the environment of the session (as established through the use of options specified with the STRSQL command).
2=EXIT WITHOUT SAVING SESSION	Terminates the Interactive SQL session without saving the environment of the session.
3=RESUME SESSION	Returns to the Interactive SQL session.

4=SAVE SESSION IN SOURCE FILE   Saves the current session in a source
                                       file as defined in the Change Source
                                       File display screen when the Enter
                                       key is pressed.

> **TIP**   Option 2 is a clean way to exit. Don't worry; all of the collections, tables,
> and data created or stored are saved. What are not saved are the statements that were
> entered and the environment of the session as it was established by the parameters
> of the STRSQL command.

After you choose an exit option and press the Enter key, the menu screen from which you started your interactive SQL session will appear.

THE AS/400 SIGN-OFF PROCESS

The AS/400 system is exited by choosing option 90 (SIGN OFF) from the MAIN MENU. If the MAIN MENU is currently displayed on the screen, type "90" at the command prompt and then press the Enter key.

```
   mm/dd/yy                 NVCC AS/400 ANNANDALE          hh:mm:ss

                        **   NVCC AS/400 SIGNOFF   **


      USERID: XXXXXXX           name of user


      TERMID: XXXXXX


           LAST SIGNON: mm/dd/yy AT hh:mm.ss

              USER TYPE: *PGMR






              **  PRESS ENTER TO LOGOFF  **

```

Figure 3.7   AS/400 NVCC Sign-Off Screen

> **TIP** If a menu other than the MAIN MENU is currently on the screen, then enter
> the command
>
> ====>GO MAIN

At this point the sign-off process may vary, depending on how your system was installed. For example, the system may respond with a screen such as the one depicted in Figure 3.7. If so, as the message on the bottom of the screen suggests, press the Enter key to end your session on the AS/400.

SUMMARY

The first step in starting an Interactive SQL session is to sign on to the AS/400 system. The sign-on process will vary, depending on your system's setup. After signing on to the AS/400 system, you can start an Interactive SQL session either by choosing it as an option from the DECISION SUPPORT menu or by entering the command STRSQL at the command prompt.

The fastest way to start an interactive SQL session is to enter the STRSQL command at the command prompt. Although you may enter the STRSQL command without any additional information, the command offers a number of parameters that allow you to specify particular processing options.

The function keys that are defined on the bottom of the Interactive SQL screen differ somewhat from those on the AS/400 menu screens. They include F3, F4, F6, F9, F10, F12, F13, and F24. If you press F24 (MORE KEYS), your selection of function keys changes to include F14, F15, F16, F17, F18, and F24. These function keys, as well as some others that are not displayed on the screen, are available for your use.

To terminate an Interactive SQL session and return to the menu system of the AS/400 (from which you may exit the AS/400 system), simply press function key three (F3), as noted on the bottom of the Interactive SQL screen. Sign off from the AS/400 system by choosing option 90 (SIGN OFF) on the AS/400 MAIN MENU.

ENDNOTE

1. *Application System/400 Systems Application Architecture Structured Query Language/400 Programmer's Guide (SC41-9609-03), Version 2,* IBM Corporation, 4th ed. (November 1993), pp. D-94 and D-95.

QUESTIONS

1. How do you start an Interactive SQL session on the AS/400?

2. What does it mean to "enter a command"?

3. Which AS/400 command menu has Interactive SQL as an option?

4. Instead of selecting the menu option INTERACTIVE SQL, is there a benefit to using the STRSQL command to start an Interactive SQL session?

5. How might the GO command be used in starting an Interactive SQL session?

6. How do the function keys in an Interactive SQL session differ from those on the AS/400 command menus?

7. What is the purpose of function key one (F1)?

8. How do you end an Interactive SQL session on the AS/400?

9. Why is option 2 on the Exit Interactive SQL screen a reasonable, if not preferred, way to terminate an Interactive SQL session?

10. Does terminating an Interactive SQL session equate to signing off the AS/400 system?

EXERCISES

1. Locate a terminal or work station that has access to an AS/400. Sign on to the AS/400 system. Begin with the AS/400 MAIN MENU and traverse through the menus, ultimately selecting the option to start an Interactive SQL session. Exit the Interactive SQL session. Use the STRSQL command to start another Interactive SQL session. Contrast the two approaches.

2. Type STRSQL at an AS/400 command line and then press F1 (HELP). Study the information provided by the help feature. Start an Interactive SQL session and then press F1 (HELP). Is the information provided by the help feature different? Continue to experiment with the help feature.

4

Interactive

Database Creation

CONSTRUCTING A DATA MODEL

The first task in creating a database is to determine the information processing needs of those who will use the database. A data model should be constructed to represent the processing needs and the data that support these needs. A data model is a pictorial representation of the data and the interrelationships that exist to support information processing needs.

There are three types of data models that are supported by DBMS software packages currently on the market. These are

1. the hierarchical model,
2. the network (or CODASYL) model, and
3. the relational model.

Figure 4.1 depicts the three models.

Each of these models can be used to represent data and the relationships among data. A hierarchical model represents data relationships using hierarchies, or trees. A tree is composed of a series, or classification, of elements called nodes. There are parent and child nodes. Nodes are connected by branches, which represent relationships. A definitive feature of a hierarchical model is that a node may have more than one child, but only one parent. A network model also is composed of nodes and branches, but differs from the hierarchical model in that one or more nodes may have multiple parents. The network model is more flexible because any node may be linked to any other node. A relational model, which is composed of normalized tables, was described in detail in Chapter 1.

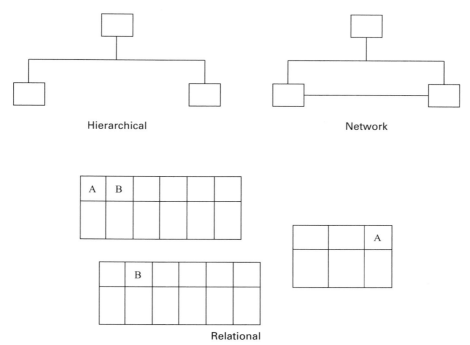

Figure 4.1   Hierarchical, Network, and Relational Data Models

A key difference in the models is the way the relationships are implemented. In both the hierarchical and network models, relationships are maintained separately from the data. Link fields (pointers), maps, or some other form of storage is maintained to represent the relationships. In the relational model there are no separate link fields or structures. The relationships are maintained within the data, and relational operators are used to relate the data.

Figure 4.2 illustrates a relational data model that we will implement using Interactive SQL on the AS/400. The model, as introduced in Chapter 1, represents a medical organization's data on surgeries performed (admittedly a very narrow view).

THE CREATE COLLECTION STATEMENT

The first step in using SQL on the AS/400 to implement the relational database model depicted in Figure 4.2 is to define the object that will be used to store the collection of tables, views, and indexes that is created in support of the model. The CREATE COLLECTION statement is used for this purpose. The storage of data on the AS/400 is accomplished through the use of libraries (see Appendix B). The AS/400 storage term LIBRARY is synonymous with the AS/400 SQL term COLLECTION.

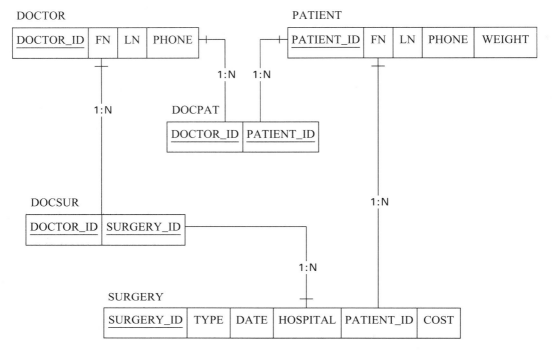

Figure 4.2   Example of Relational Data Model for MEDICAL Database

The syntax of the CREATE COLLECTION statement is

```
CREATE COLLECTION collection-name
```

The collection's name should conform to the standard library naming conventions of the installation. Like other identifiers' names, the name must abide by the following restrictions:

1. The maximum length is ten characters.
2. The identifier must start with a letter followed by zero or more characters, each of which is a letter, a digit, or the underscore character.
3. The identifier must not be a reserved word.

Use of the CREATE COLLECTION Statement

You would start the process of implementing the database model in Figure 4.2 by proceeding to the Interactive SQL screen (as described in Chapter 3) and entering the command

```
===>CREATE COLLECTION MEDICAL
```

As the system creates your collection it keeps you informed of its progress by flashing on the bottom of the screen messages concerning its work in building the paths and system files needed to support an SQL database.

	`JUNKANDMOR TOO LONG. MAXIMUM 10 CHARACTERS.`
	Entering a statement such as
	`CREATE COLLECTION JUNKANDMOREJUNK`
	results in the above error message. To correct the statement, specify a collection name that has no more than ten characters in it.
BOO **BOO** **BOX**	
	`TOKEN - WAS NOT VALID. VALID TOKENS: <END-OF-STATEMENT>.`
	Entering a statement such as
	`CREATE COLLECTION JUN---@@K`
	results in the above error message. To correct the statement, specify a collection name that is composed of valid characters (A–Z, 0–9, and the underscore).

AS/400 Prompt Feature (F4) to Create a Collection

An alternative to entering the CREATE COLLECTION statement at the Interactive SQL prompt is to use the prompting feature (F4) of the AS/400. The previous definition of the MEDICAL collection could have been accomplished by using the prompting feature as follows.

In the Interactive SQL screen, type the statement CREATE and then press function key four (F4), instead of pressing the Enter key.

BOO **BOO** **BOX**	`TOKEN <END-OF-STATEMENT> WAS NOT VALID. VALID TOKENS:` Pressing the Enter key instead of F4 will yield the above error message. To correct the error, simply press the F4 key, *not* the Enter key.

When you press F4, the SELECT CREATE STATEMENT screen illustrated in Figure 4.3 is displayed. Type a "1" and then press the Enter key. The SPECIFY CREATE COLLECTION STATEMENT screen illustrated in Figure 4.4 is displayed. The word "NAME," just to the right of the cursor, means that you must enter a valid name for your collection. Type a valid collection name, such as MEDICAL, and then press the Enter key. As the system creates your collection it keeps you informed of its progress by flashing messages on the bottom of the screen.

```
                       SELECT CREATE STATEMENT

   SELECT ONE OF THE FOLLOWING:

           1. CREATE COLLECTION
           2. CREATE INDEX
           3. CREATE TABLE
           4. CREATE VIEW




   SELECTION
   _

   F3=EXIT    F4=CANCEL
```

Figure 4.3   SELECT CREATE STATEMENT Screen

```
                 SPECIFY CREATE COLLECTION STATEMENT

   TYPE CHOICE, PRESS ENTER.

      LIBRARY ............_                    NAME








   F3=EXIT   F5=REFRESH   F12=CANCEL   F21=DISPLAY STATEMENT
```

Figure 4.4   SPECIFY CREATE COLLECTION STATEMENT Screen

Note: Copyrighted screens in this chapter are used by permission of IBM Corporation.

```
CREATE TABLE collection-name/table-name

(column-name data-type │ NOT NULL
                       │ NOT NULL WITH DEFAULT │FOR BIT DATA   │
                                               │FOR SBCS DATA  │
                                               │FOR MIXED DATA │

 ┌                  ┐
 │ , column-name... │   )
 └                  ┘
```

Figure 4.5   Syntax of the CREATE TABLE Command

THE CREATE TABLE STATEMENT

After you have defined the object that will be used to store the collection of tables, views, and indexes, you can define the tables. The CREATE TABLE statement is used to define a database table. On the AS/400, a database table is a physical file that will store the actual user data. Figure 4.5 outlines the syntax of the CREATE TABLE statement.

Recall from our discussion of the relational database approach in Chapter 1 that any table that is a part of a relational database must abide by a set of rules. Although the CREATE TABLE statement does not enforce all of the rules discussed, its syntax is best understood in reference to the rules. The syntax of the CREATE TABLE statement requires a unique name for each column (a table name follows the same restrictions as a collection name), thus supporting the rule that each column must have a distinct name.

The data type specifies what type of data will be stored in the column. The syntax of the CREATE TABLE statement allows for only one data type to be specified per column, thus supporting the rule that all data items within a column must be of the same data type. Your choices for data type on the AS/400 include the following:[1]

INTEGER or INT	for a large integer
SMALLINT	for a small integer
FLOAT	for a floating-point number
REAL	for single-precision floating-point number
DOUBLE PRECISION	for a double-precision floating-point number
DECIMAL or DEC	for a packed decimal number
NUMERIC	for a zoned decimal number
CHARACTER or CHAR	for a fixed-length character string
VARCHAR (integer)	for a varying-length character string of maximum length integer (1–32,740)
DATE	for a date
TIME	for a time
TIMESTAMP	for a timestamp

GRAPHIC (integer)   for a fixed-length graphic string of length integer
                                       (1–16,383)

VARGRAPHIC (integer)   for a varying-length graphic string of maximum
                                       length integer (1–16,370)

The qualifiers that are used in specifying a data type include the following:

NOT NULL   Prevents the column from containing null values.

NOT NULL WITH DEFAULT   Prevents the column from containing null values
                                       and allows a default value other than the null value.
                                       The default value used depends on the data type of
                                       the column. For numeric data types the default
                                       value is zero; for the character data type the default
                                       value is blanks.

NOT NULL WITH DEFAULT
FOR BIT DATA   Specifies that the character (CHAR) column con-
                                       tains hex data.

NOT NULL WITH DEFAULT
FOR SBCS DATA   Specifies that the character column contains single-
                                       byte character set (SBCS) data. FOR SBCS DATA
                                       is the default for CHAR columns.

NOT NULL WITH DEFAULT
FOR MIXED DATA   Specifies that the character column contains both
                                       SBCS data and double-byte character set (DBCS)
                                       data. FOR MIXED DBCS is the default for CHAR
                                       columns if the system is DBCS-capable and the
                                       length of the column is greater than 3. If the system
                                       is not DBCS-capable and FOR MIXED DATA is
                                       specified, an error occurs.

The rule that a column (or select group of columns) must be identified as a key for
the table is in part supported by these qualifiers. For example, by specifying that a column's data type be NOT NULL, we force the user to place some value (which may be used
as a key) into the defined column.

Use of the CREATE TABLE Statement

To continue the process of implementing the database model depicted in Figure 4.2 at the
Interactive SQL screen, enter each of the following CREATE statements separately:

```
===>CREATE TABLE MEDICAL/DOCTOR
        (DOCTOR_ID   CHAR(4)     NOT NULL,
         FN          CHAR(10)    NOT NULL WITH DEFAULT,
         LN          CHAR(10)    NOT NULL WITH DEFAULT,
         PHONE       CHAR(8)     NOT NULL WITH DEFAULT)
```

> **TIP**   Use the Return key to move the cursor down a line on the screen when typing the statement; press the Enter key only after the entire statement has been typed.

> **TIP**   After entering the above CREATE TABLE statement, you can save yourself some typing on the next CREATE TABLE by using the retrieve function of F9. With the cursor located at the prompt, press F9. The last statement executed (CREATE TABLE MEDICAL/DOCTOR) is displayed. Use the arrow keys to move the cursor to the appropriate locations, and type over the word DOCTOR with PATIENT.

```
===>CREATE TABLE MEDICAL/PATIENT
        (PATIENT_ID   CHAR(4)     NOT NULL,
         FN           CHAR(10)    NOT NULL WITH DEFAULT,
         LN           CHAR(10)    NOT NULL WITH DEFAULT,
         PHONE        CHAR(8)     NOT NULL WITH DEFAULT,
         WEIGHT       NUMERIC(3)  NOT NULL WITH DEFAULT)

===>CREATE TABLE MEDICAL/SURGERY
        (SURGERY_ID   CHAR(4)       NOT NULL,
         TYPE         CHAR(10)      NOT NULL WITH DEFAULT,
         DATE         CHAR(10)      NOT NULL WITH DEFAULT,
         HOSPITAL     CHAR(15)      NOT NULL WITH DEFAULT,
         PATIENT_ID   CHAR(4)       NOT NULL WITH DEFAULT,
         COST         NUMERIC(7,2)  NOT NULL WITH DEFAULT)

===>CREATE TABLE MEDICAL/DOCSUR
        (DOCTOR_ID    CHAR(4)  NOT NULL,
         SURGERY_ID   CHAR(4)  NOT NULL)

===>CREATE TABLE MEDICAL/DOCPAT
        (DOCTOR_ID    CHAR(4)  NOT NULL,
         PATIENT_ID   CHAR(4)  NOT NULL)
```

> **BOO BOO BOX**   Since there is no statement available in AS/400 Interactive SQL to modify the structure of a table once it has been created, if you make a mistake in defining the table you must delete (drop) the table and then re-create it correctly. See the discussion on the use of the DROP STATEMENT later in this chapter.

AS/400 Prompt Feature (F4) to Create a Table

An alternative to entering the CREATE TABLE statement at the Interactive SQL prompt is to use the prompting feature (F4) of the AS/400.

TIP If you would like to practice with the prompt feature to create a table but have already defined each of the tables in the example MEDICAL database, then enter the following DROP statement before proceeding:

```
===>DROP TABLE MEDICAL/PATIENT
```

The definition of the PATIENT table might have been accomplished by using the prompting feature as follows. At the Interactive SQL screen, type the statement CREATE and then press function key four (F4) instead of pressing the Enter key. The SELECT CREATE STATEMENT screen illustrated in Figure 4.3 is presented. Type a "3" and then press the Enter key. The early release of the AS/400 system presents the SPECIFY CRE-ATE TABLE STATEMENT screen illustrated in Figure 4.6; later releases of the AS/400 system present the screen illustrated in Figure 4.7. Let's first look at the screen presented in the early release (Figure 4.6).

```
                    SPECIFY CREATE TABLE STATEMENT

    TYPE CHOICES.

        FILE . . . . . . . . . . . . .  _           NAME
        LIBRARY . . . . . . . . . .                 NAME, F4 FOR LIST

    TYPE INFORMATION, PRESS ENTER.
      DEFAULT:    Y=YES, N=NO
      DATA:       1=BIT, 2=SBCS, 3=MIXED

                          -----DIGITS-----
    FIELD       TYPE      PRECISION  SCALE  LENGTH  DEFAULT   DATA
                                                       Y        2
                                                       Y        2
                                                       Y        2
                                                       Y        2
                                                       Y        2
                                                       Y        2
                                                       Y        2


    F3=EXIT   F4=PROMPT F5=REFRESH F6=INSERT LINE   F10=COPY LINE
    F12=CANCEL F14=DELETE LINE F21=DISPLAY STATEMENT
```

Figure 4.6   SPECIFY CREATE TABLE STATEMENT Screen (Early AS/400 System Version)

The word "NAME," just to the right of the cursor in Figure 4.6, means you must enter a valid name for your table. Type in a valid table name, such as PATIENT, and then press the Return key or the Tab key (*not* the Enter key).

TIP Use the Tab key to move from field to field and the Return key to move from line to line. Press the Enter key only after you have typed in entries for all screen items.

Next you must type the name of the collection (library) that will store the table. As suggested to the right of the cursor, you could press the F4 key and let the system provide a list of names from which to choose. Type a valid collection name, such as MEDICAL, and then press the Return key or the Tab key (*not* the Enter key).

TIP   If your library (collection) name does not appear in the list of names provided using F4, then it is not a member of your session library list. You can just type in the library name. To include a library on your session library list, you can issue the AS/400 CL command ADDLLIBLE. For example, when you are at the AS/400 command prompt (prior to starting your next Interactive SQL session), enter the command

```
          SELECTION OR COMMAND
          ===>ADDLIBLE MEDICAL
```

With the cursor under the title FIELD, type a valid field name, such as PATIENT_ID, and then press the Tab key. With the cursor under the title TYPE, type a valid data type, such as CHAR, and then press the Tab key. The cursor should now be under the title PRECISION, within the DIGITS section.

The DIGITS section is used for numeric data types; the LENGTH entry is used for CHAR data types. The PRECISION entry defines the number of total digits in the field. The SCALE entry defines the number of digits to the right of an implied decimal point. The LENGTH entry defines the length of a CHAR field—that is, the maximum number of characters that will be stored in the field. If you had specified a numeric data type, you would use the DIGITS columns to define its precision (and optionally its scale), but define no LENGTH value. If you had specified the CHAR data type, you would use LENGTH, but not DIGITS.

For example, suppose you are entering the WEIGHT field, with a numeric data type. With the cursor under the title PRECISION, type a number, such as "3", and then press the Tab key. The weight field does not need decimal digits, so press the Tab key again. The cursor moves under the title LENGTH. Since you specified a numeric data type, you cannot define a LENGTH value. To accept the default values for DEFAULT and DATA, press the Tab key three times (or press the Return key). The cursor will move under the title FIELD, just below the last field defined.

BOO BOO BOX	INCORRECT COMBINATION OF PARAMETERS SPECIFIED This is the error message you will see in some versions if you specify a numeric data type and enter a value for LENGTH, or if you specify a CHAR data type and enter a value for DIGITS, or if you enter a value for both DIGITS and LENGTH for a field. Remember, only CHAR type fields have LENGTH defined (with no DIGITS defined).

```
                    SPECIFY CREATE TABLE STATEMENT

  TYPE CHOICES.

    FILE .............. _                NAME
      LIBRARY ........                   NAME, F4 FOR LIST

  TYPE INFORMATION, PRESS ENTER.
    NULLS:  1=NULL, 2=NOT NULL, 3=NOT NULL WITH DEFAULT
    DATA:   1=BIT, 2=SBCS, 3=MIXED, 4=CCSID

  FIELD     TYPE     LENGTH  SCALE  NULLS  DATA  ALLOCATE CCSID
                                      3
                                      3
                                      3
                                      3
                                      3
                                      3
                                      3


  F3=EXIT   F4=PROMPT F5=REFRESH F6=INSERT LINE   F10=COPY LINE
  F12=CANCEL F14=DELETE LINE F21=DISPLAY STATEMENT
```

Figure 4.7   SPECIFY CREATE TABLE STATEMENT Screen (Later AS/400 System Version)

```
                    SPECIFY CREATE TABLE STATEMENT

  TYPE CHOICES.

    FILE .............. patient          NAME
    LIBRARY .......... medical           NAME, F4 FOR LIST

  TYPE INFORMATION, PRESS ENTER.
    DEFAULT:   Y=YES, N=NO
    DATA:      1=BIT, 2=SBCS, 3=MIXED

                         -----DIGITS-----
  FIELD       TYPE     PRECISION  SCALE  LENGTH  DEFAULT  DATA
  patient_id  char                         4        Y      2
  fn          char                        10        Y      2
  ln          char                        10        Y      2
  phone       char                         8        Y      2
  weight      numeric  3                            Y      2
                                                    Y      2
                                                    Y      2

  F3=EXIT   F4=PROMPT F5=REFRESH F6=INSERT LINE   F10=COPY LINE
  F12=CANCEL F14=DELETE LINE F21=DISPLAY STATEMENT
```

Figure 4.8   Example of Completed SPECIFY CREATE TABLE STATEMENT Screen

In the later releases of the AS/400 System, the SPECIFY CREATE TABLE SCREEN was modified (see Figure 4.7). Note that the PRECISION and DEFAULT columns have been removed. The LENGTH field is used to specify the length, and the SCALE field is used to specify digits to the right of the decimal.

Complete the definition of the PATIENT table by simply repeating the steps and entering the remaining fields for the table. When you have finished, your screen should resemble the one in Figure 4.8. Once you have typed in all of the information, press the Enter key.

THE CREATE VIEW STATEMENT

A database integrates functions and may serve many users. Although the database has a single physical form (defined through the use of the CREATE COLLECTION and CREATE TABLE statements), not all users may perceive the same form. For reasons of security or functional segregation, it may be appropriate to limit what some users see as the database to just those items relevant to their particular needs.

Views, as discussed in Chapter 1, provide a way to logically dissect the physical database. In that chapter we considered the situation in which the cost associated with a surgery is restricted information, but data on the types of surgeries by date and hospital should be available to all users. The CREATE VIEW statement defines a different way to look at the existing SURGERY table, so that some users cannot access the cost data.

Figure 4.9 illustrates the syntax of the CREATE VIEW statement. A view name follows the same restrictions as a collection name or a table name. A view cannot reference more than 8000 columns or more than 32 real tables. A list of one or more column names is optional. If you specify a list, then be sure to include as many names as there are columns in the subselect. The subselect portion of the statement actually defines the view; it selects which columns will be included from the specified table(s). The rules that apply to selecting data in response to a query, discussed in Chapter 6, also apply to the specification of the subselect portion of the CREATE VIEW statement.

```
CREATE VIEW collection-name/view-name  ⌈column-name, ...⌉  AS subselect
```

Figure 4.9 Syntax of the CREATE VIEW Statement

Note: The subselect must be a valid SELECT statement (see Chapter 6).

Use of the CREATE VIEW Statement

To create a view that excludes the cost data, you would proceed to the Interactive SQL screen and enter the statement

```
===>CREATE VIEW MEDICAL/OPS (SURGERY_ID, TYPE, DATE, HOSPITAL,
     PATIENT_ID) AS SELECT SURGERY_ID, TYPE, DATE, HOSPITAL,
     PATIENT_ID FROM MEDICAL/SURGERY
```

AS/400 Prompt Feature (F4) to Create a View

An alternative to entering the CREATE VIEW command at the Interactive SQL prompt is to use the prompting feature (F4) of the AS/400.

TIP   If you would like to practice with the prompt feature to create a view but have already defined the OPS view in the MEDICAL database example, then enter the following DROP statement before proceeding:

```
===>DROP VIEW MEDICAL/OPS
```

The definition of the OPS table (view) could have been accomplished by using the prompting feature as follows. At the Interactive SQL screen, type the statement CREATE and then press function key four (F4) instead of pressing the Enter key.

BOO BOO BOX	TOKEN <END-OF-STATEMENT> WAS NOT VALID. VALID TOKENS: Pressing the Enter key instead of F4 will yield the above error message. To correct the error, simply press the F4 key, *not* the Enter key.

The SELECT CREATE STATEMENT screen illustrated in Figure 4.3 will be displayed. Type a "4" and then press the Enter key. The SPECIFY CREATE VIEW STATEMENT screen illustrated in Figure 4.10 will be displayed. The word "NAME," just to the right of the cursor, reminds you that you must enter a valid name for your view. Type a valid table name, such as OPS, and then press the Return key or the Tab key (*not* the Enter key).

Next you must type the name of the collection (library) in which you wish the logical table to be stored. As suggested to the right of the cursor, you could press the F4 key and let the system provide a list of names from which to choose. Type a valid collection name, such as MEDICAL, and then press the Tab key.

The FIELD NAMES FOR VIEW prompt offers you two choices. The first (and default) option specifies that the field names of the view that you are defining should be the same as those that currently exist in the table from which the view will be built. The second option (type a "2" to pick this option) specifies that you wish to identify new field names. If you select this option, be careful to enter the same number of names in the next screen as there will be fields resulting from your select. In our example, we will accept the default by pressing the Enter key. A second SPECIFY CREATE VIEW STATEMENT screen, as illustrated in Figure 4.11, will be displayed.

Type MEDICAL/SURGERY as a response to the FROM FILES prompt, and then advance the cursor to the SELECT FIELDS prompt. With the cursor flashing next to the SELECT FIELDS prompt, type the names of the desired fields (SURGERY_ID, TYPE, DATE, HOSPITAL, PATIENT_ID), as shown in Figure 4.12. Press the Enter key (accepting the default NO answer to distinct records), and the system will process your request and create a view.

```
                    SPECIFY CREATE VIEW STATEMENT

  TYPE CHOICES, PRESS ENTER.

     VIEW .............. _                    NAME
         LIBRARY ........                     NAME, F4 FOR LIST

     FIELD NAMES FOR VIEW ....1                1=USE RESULT
                                                 FILE NAMES
                                               2=SPECIFY NAMES












  F3=EXIT F4=PROMPT F5=REFRESH F12=CANCEL F21=DISPLAY STATEMENT
```

Figure 4.10   SPECIFY CREATE VIEW STATEMENT (First) Screen

```
                    SPECIFY CREATE VIEW STATEMENT

  TYPE SUBSELECT INFORMATION. PRESS F4 FOR A LIST.

     FROM FILES ........._

     SELECT FIELDS .......

     WHERE CONDITIONS ...

     GROUP BY FIELDS ....

     HAVING CONDITIONS ..


  TYPE CHOICE, PRESS ENTER.

     DISTINCT RECORDS IN RESULT FILE .......N  Y=YES, N=NO

  F3=EXIT F4=PROMPT F5=REFRESH F6=INSERT LINE F10=COPY LINE
  F12=CANCEL     F24=MORE KEYS
```

Figure 4.11   SPECIFY CREATE VIEW STATEMENT (Second) Screen

Refer to the discussion on the SELECT statement in Chapters 6, 7, and 8 to gain perspective on the optional use of the WHERE CONDITIONS, GROUP BY FIELDS, and HAVING CONDITIONS options.

```
                SPECIFY CREATE VIEW STATEMENT

    TYPE SUBSELECT INFORMATION. PRESS F4 FOR A LIST.

       FROM FILES ........MEDICAL/SURGERY

       SELECT FIELDS ....SURGERY_ID,TYPE,DATE,HOSPITAL,PATIENT_ID

       WHERE CONDITIONS ...

       GROUP BY FIELDS ....

       HAVING CONDITIONS ..


    TYPE CHOICE, PRESS ENTER.

       DISTINCT RECORDS IN RESULT FILE .......N   Y=YES, N=NO

    F3=EXIT F4=PROMPT F5=REFRESH F6=INSERT LINE F10=COPY LINE
    F12=CANCEL      F24=MORE KEYS
```

Figure 4.12   Sample of Completed SPECIFY CREATE VIEW STATEMENT (Second) Screen

THE CREATE INDEX STATEMENT

An SQL index is a file created to maintain an ordered accounting of the data contained in a database file (table) based on one or more columns of the database file (table). Indexes are optional, but they can increase the speed of data retrieval when dealing with large

```
    CREATE | UNIQUE                  |  INDEX   index-name
           | UNIQUE WHERE NOT NULL   |

           ON   collection-name/table-name

           (column-name  | ASC  |
                         | DESC |


           | , column-name... |  )
```

Figure 4.13   Syntax of the CREATE INDEX Statement

tables (for example, when ordering 1000 or more rows). An index allows the system to retrieve data without having to access all of the data in a table.

Indexes created in Interactive SQL are referenced and maintained automatically by the system. In addition, any number of indexes may be created, and indexes may be created or dropped at any time. Figure 4.13 illustrates the syntax of the CREATE INDEX statement.

Use of the CREATE INDEX Statement

An index is created by executing the CREATE INDEX statement. For example, to create an index that supports the retrieval of data on surgeries ordered by hospital name, enter the statement

```
===>CREATE INDEX HOSPNDX1 ON MEDICAL/SURGERY (HOSPITAL)
```

In our example, HOSPNDX1 names the index. You may give the index any name you like (following the same rules as for naming collections), but you cannot use the name of an index, table, or view that already exists. The clause ON MEDICAL/SURGERY identifies the table to be indexed. The column on which the table is to be indexed is identified in parentheses. In our example we create an index on HOSPITAL data in the SURGERY table. The index HOSPNDX1 will be used by the system whenever we request information from the SURGERY table ordered by hospital name.

You may create an index that orders the data on more than one column. For example, you could create an index based on types of surgeries within hospitals with a statement such as

```
===>CREATE INDEX HOSPNDX2
        ON MEDICAL/SURGERY (HOSPITAL, TYPE)
```

For each column you may specify whether the index entries should be in ascending (ASC) or descending (DESC) order. (Ascending is the default.) You may also employ the keyword UNIQUE to prevent the table from containing two or more rows of data with the same index value. For example, you could enter

```
===>CREATE UNIQUE INDEX HOSPNDX3
        ON MEDICAL/SURGERY (SURGERY_ID)
```

BOO BOO BOX	UNIQUE INDEX CANNOT BE CREATED BECAUSE OF DUPLICATE KEYS. Specifying that the index be UNIQUE on a column that holds duplicate data values will result in the above error message. A UNIQUE index cannot be created on a table that contains duplicate key values.

If the table named in the CREATE INDEX statement contains data, then the index entries are created when you execute the CREATE INDEX command. If the table does not contain data at the time the CREATE INDEX statement is executed, then the CREATE INDEX statement simply creates a description of the index. You cannot create a UNIQUE index before data are entered. Index entries are automatically updated by the system when data are entered into the table or when the data in the table are modified.

THE DROP STATEMENT

The DROP statement is used to delete a collection, base table, index table, or view.
    The syntax of the DROP statement is

```
          | COLLECTION collection-name |
          | TABLE table-name           |
   DROP   | INDEX index-table-name     |
          | VIEW view-name             |
          | PACKAGE package-name       |
```

When a collection is dropped, all of the objects (tables, indexes, and so forth) that are a part of the collection are deleted. When a table is dropped, all indexes, views, data, and logical files defined on the table are deleted.

Use of the DROP Statement

Because a table cannot be modified once it has been created, the DROP statement is the only means by which to correct a definition error. Simply stated, the mistake-laden table is deleted (using the DROP statement) and then re-created (using the CREATE TABLE statement). Thus, it is best to check and then double check a created structure for correctness before entering actual data into it.
    The statement that would delete the DOCTOR table is

```
   ===>DROP TABLE MEDICAL/DOCTOR
```

SUMMARY

A data model is a pictorial representation of the user's data requirements. There are three types of data models that are supported by DBMS software packages currently on the market: the hierarchical model, the network (or CODASYL) model, and the relational model.
    SQL on the AS/400 supports the relational data model. The first step in using SQL on the AS/400 to implement a relational database model is to define the object that will be used to store the collection of tables, views, and indexes to support the model. The CREATE COLLECTION statement is used for this purpose.
    Once you have defined the object, you define the tables. The CREATE TABLE statement is used to define a database table. On the AS/400, a database table is a physical file that will store the actual user data.
    A database integrates functions and may serve many users. Although the database has a single physical form (defined through the use of the CREATE COLLECTION and CREATE TABLE statements), not all users may perceive the same form. Views are logical dissections of the physical database. A view contains no actual data, but instead is a redefinition of another table (or collection of tables). The CREATE VIEW statement is used to create alternative views of existing database tables.
    The DROP statement is used to delete tables, collections, indexes, and views. Because a table cannot be modified, the only way to deal with a mistake-laden table is to delete it with the DROP statement and then re-create it with the CREATE TABLE state-

ment. Thus, it is very important to make sure the created structure is correct before entering actual data into it.

ENDNOTE

1. *Application System/400 Systems Application Architecture Structured Query Language/400 Reference (SC41-9608-03), Version 2*, IBM Corporation, 4th ed. (November 1993), pp. 196–198.

QUESTIONS

1. What is a data model? Why is it important?
2. What are the three types of data models that are supported by DBMS software packages currently on the market?
3. In Figure 4.2, what is the relationship between the DOCTOR table and the SURGERY table? Discuss what the relationship implies.
4. How do the various AS/400 Interactive SQL CREATE statements support the relational database model?
5. What restrictions exist in naming collections and tables?
6. In using the prompting feature of the AS/400, why is it important to press F4 instead of pressing the Enter key?
7. What are the choices in Interactive SQL on the AS/400 for the data type of a column?
8. What are the qualifiers that may be used when specifying a data type of a column? Explain their relevance.
9. Define what is meant by SCALE and LENGTH in defining fields (columns). How do they relate to each other?
10. Of what use is the CREATE INDEX statement?
11. Of what use is the DROP statement?

EXERCISES

1. Create the example MEDICAL database depicted in Figure 4.2 by entering each of the example Interactive SQL statements introduced and discussed in this chapter.
2. Draw a relational database model that represents the tables required to support the information processing needs of a personnel office. The office keeps data on the identification number, name, department, and salary of employees along with data on courses (course identification number, course description, date of course) that employees complete. An employee may complete zero, one, or many courses. Code and enter the appropriate CREATE statements to establish an AS/400 database. Describe how the concept of a view may be employed to restrict access to information on the salary of an employee.
3. Research the hierarchical and network types of data models, and contrast them to the relational model.

5

Interactive
Data Maintenance
Statements

THE INSERT STATEMENT

After using the CREATE COLLECTION, CREATE TABLE, and CREATE VIEW statements to create the physical data structures that support the conceptual data model, you can load data into the structures with the INSERT statement. Two related statements, the UPDATE statement and the DELETE statement, are available to correct mistakes, revise data, or remove data that are no longer desired.

The INSERT statement loads data into a table that has been previously created with the CREATE TABLE statement or the CREATE VIEW statement. Since views contain no data of their own, but rather exist as perceived variations of existing tables, inserting data into a view actually inserts the data into the table(s) upon which the view is based.

Figure 5.1 depicts sample data for the tables that were created in support of the MEDICAL database discussed in Chapter 4. Each INSERT statement entered will add one row of data into a table.

To load the sample data provided in Figure 5.1 into the MEDICAL database (created in Chapter 4), proceed to the Interactive SQL screen. Add the first row of data into the PATIENT table by entering the statement

```
INSERT INTO MEDICAL/PATIENT (PATIENT_ID, FN, LN, PHONE, WEIGHT)
   VALUES ('2000', 'Joe', 'Dillon', '555-1212', 160)
```

An equally correct and less verbose statement that takes advantage of the implicit column list feature is

```
INSERT INTO MEDICAL/PATIENT
   VALUES ('2000','JOE','DILLON','555-1212',160)
```

DOCTOR

DOCTOR_ID	FN	LN	PHONE
1000	Joe	Smith	555-1111
1100	Ken	Peters	555-3333
1150	John·	Jones	555-4444
1200	Mary	Henry	555-5555
1250	Jason	Wright	555-6666
1300	Kevin	Doe	555-7777
1350	Teresa	Willis	555-8888

DOCPAT

DOCTOR_ID	PATIENT_ID
1000	2150
1350	2150
1300	2350
1150	2200
1200	2200
1250	2200
1000	2000
1350	2000
1100	2100
1300	2050
1350	2050

PATIENT

PATIENT_ID	FN	LN	PHONE	WEIGHT
2000	Joe	Dillon	555-1212	160
2050	Pete	Mark	555-1313	180
2100	Nancy	Smith	555-1414	120
2150	Betty	Jones	555-1515	130
2200	Frank	Lamb	555-1616	210
2250	Mike	Post	555-1717	145
2300	Sam	Parken	555-1818	220
2350	Abby	Pearl	555-1919	105
2400	Alice	Able	555-1010	160

DOCSUR

DOCTOR_ID	SURGERY_ID
1000	3000
1350	3000
1300	3010
1150	3100
1200	3100
1250	3100
1000	3150
1350	3150
1100	3200
1300	3250
1350	3300
1300	3300

SURGERY

SURGERY_ID	TYPE	DATE	HOSPITAL	PATIENT_ID	COST
3000	Heart	10/10/92	Fairfax	2150	25000.00
3010	Cosmetic	12/31/91	Arlington	2350	5000.00
3100	Brain	11/9/92	Fairfax	2200	45000.98
3150	Heart	11/30/92	Fairfax	2000	27500.50
3200	Hernia	10/16/92	Arlington	2100	7000.45
3250	Cosmetic	10/12/92	Arlington	2350	3650.98
3300	Heart	11/2/91	Arlington	2050	35005.76

Figure 5.1   Sample Data for MEDICAL Database

Figure 5.2 illustrates the syntax of the INSERT statement. The INTO clause is required because it identifies the table or view into which the specified data values are to be entered. The list of one or more columns enclosed in parentheses is optional. If the list is omitted, the system matches the list of data values specified against an implicit list of all the columns in the order in which they exist in the referenced table or view.

```
INSERT INTO  |collection-name/table-name  |  ⌈(column-name, ...)⌉
             |collection-name/view-name   |  ⌊                  ⌋

             |constant, ...
    VALUES ( |host-variable, ...          |  )
             |special-register, ...
```

Figure 5.2   Syntax Chart for INSERT Statement

T I P   Specify column names if values are not provided for all columns. For example, if the first name (FN) of the patient and the weight are not known, the remaining data values may be entered with the statement

```
INSERT INTO MEDICAL/PATIENT (PATIENT_ID, LN, PHONE)
     VALUES ('2000', 'Dillon', '555-1212')
```

Note that the data value for WEIGHT, a numeric field, should not be enclosed in single quotation marks. Character, date, time, and timestamp type data values are enclosed in single quotes. It is important to note that single quotes, not double quotes, are used to enclose data values.

BOO BOO BOX	`TOKEN "2000" WAS NOT VALID. VALID TOKENS: + - ? :`
	`   NULL USER<FLOAT>`
	
	This error message occurs if you place double quotes around a data value you are assigning to a CHAR type field, as in
	
	`INSERT INTO MEDICAL/PATIENT`
	`   VALUES ("2000","Joe","Dillon","555-1212",160)`
	
	To correct the error, change the double quotes to single quotes.

Quote marks are used to delimit data. Do not confuse the use of quote marks in an Interactive SQL statement with the punctuation rules of English. 'Joe,' may be good grammar, but will generate an error message. Interactive SQL expects 'Joe',.

Use of Function Key Nine (F9) to Retrieve the Last Statement Entered

Each INSERT statement entered will add one row of data into a table. Entering numerous rows of data into a table becomes a typing challenge. Fortunately the AS/400 has a feature that minimizes the amount of typing required to enter statements that are similar in content—function key nine (F9).

Function key nine allows for the retrieval of the last statement entered. Since only the data values will change—not the syntax of the statement or the table referenced—retrieving the last INSERT statement entered and replacing its data values with those for the next row (next patient) reduces the typing requirement.

Press function key nine, and the last statement entered will appear on the screen. This should be the INSERT statement just entered to add data on the first patient. Use the arrow keys to position the cursor under the value for PATIENT_ID. Type over this value, replacing it with the value for PATIENT_ID in the next row of data in the PATIENT table. Continue to type over the data values to enter the next row of data (the next patient). The Delete key may be used to remove unwanted characters, or the Insert key may be used to insert additional characters. While typing over characters, be sure to include any required commas or quotation marks. When you have completed your editing, press the Enter key to execute the new INSERT statement.

AS/400 Prompt Feature (F4) to Insert Data

An alternative to typing the entire INSERT statement and then entering it at the Interactive SQL prompt is to use the prompting feature (F4) of the AS/400. To use the prompting feature to add data to the PATIENT table, for example, type the statement INSERT and then press function key four (F4) (instead of the Enter key).

The SPECIFY INSERT STATEMENT screen illustrated in Figure 5.3 will be displayed. The word "NAME," just to the right of the cursor, means your first option is to type a valid table (file) name. Another option, also suggested to the right of the cursor, is to press the F4 key and let the system provide you with a list of table names.

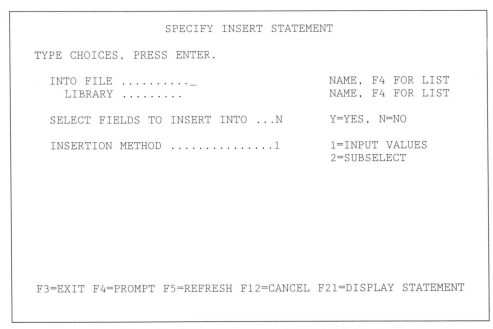

Figure 5.3   SPECIFY INSERT STATEMENT First Screen

Note: Copyrighted screens in this chapter are used by permission of IBM Corporation.

To enter our example, type the valid table name PATIENT and then press the Return key (*not* the Enter key).

TIP   Use the Return key to move from field to field. Press the Enter key only after you have typed entries for all screen items.

Next you must define the name of the collection (library) where the table is stored. Again, the message to the right of the cursor means that you can type a valid collection name or press the F4 key and let the system provide you with a list of names. To continue our example, type the valid collection name MEDICAL and then press the Return Key (*not* the Enter key).

TIP   If your library (collection) name does not appear in the list of names provided using F4, then it is not a member of your session library list. To include a library on your session library list, you can issue the AS/400 CL command ADDLIBLE. For example, anytime you are at the AS/400 command prompt, enter the command

```
SELECTION OR COMMAND
===>ADDLIBLE MEDICAL
```

The next prompt asks whether you prefer to select particular fields into which you will insert data. (The default is "N," for no, which should be used if you wish to insert data into all of the fields in the named table.) Type a "Y" and then press the Enter key. By this action you accept the default choice to the next prompt, to input values rather than use the SUBSELECT method. A description of the structure for the selected table will be displayed. Figure 5.4 illustrates the screen presented for the PATIENT table.

The cursor is located under the sequence (SEQ) column heading, to the left of the first field. For each field into which you wish to insert data, type a consecutive number, in the range from 1 to 999, in the SEQ column to the left of the desired field. If you do not number a field, it will not be included in the subsequent data entry screen. Fields do not have to be in a certain order; you could number FN as 1, LN as 2, and PATIENT_ID as 3, if you wanted them to appear in that order. To continue our example of entering data into the PATIENT table, number the fields as depicted in Figure 5.5 and then press the Enter key. The data entry screen illustrated in Figure 5.6 will be displayed. Because we chose to include each field, we could have obtained the same result by entering "N" at the SELECT FIELDS TO INSERT INTO prompt on the screen in Figure 5.3, thus skipping the screen in Figure 5.4.

Type the data for the next patient, as illustrated in Figure 5.7, and then press the Enter key.

```
                    SPECIFY INSERT STATEMENT

TYPE SEQUENCE NUMBERS (1-999) TO MAKE SELECTIONS, PRESS ENTER.

SEQ   FIELD         TYPE        DIGITS   LENGTH NULLS
  _   PATIENT_ID    CHARACTER              4 NOT NULL
      FN            CHARACTER             10 NOT NULL WITH DEFAULT
      LN            CHARACTER             10 NOT NULL WITH DEFAULT
      PHONE         CHARACTER              8 NOT NULL WITH DEFAULT
      WEIGHT        NUMERIC      3           NOT NULL WITH DEFAULT




                                                            BOTTOM

   F3=EXIT      F5=REFRESH      F12=CANCEL     F21=DISPLAY STATEMENT
```

Figure 5.4 SPECIFY INSERT STATEMENT Second Screen

```
                    SPECIFY INSERT STATEMENT

TYPE SEQUENCE NUMBERS (1-999) TO MAKE SELECTIONS, PRESS ENTER.

SEQ   FIELD         TYPE        DIGITS   LENGTH NULLS
  1   PATIENT_ID    CHARACTER              4 NOT NULL
  2   FN            CHARACTER             10 NOT NULL WITH DEFAULT
  3   LN            CHARACTER             10 NOT NULL WITH DEFAULT
  4   PHONE         CHARACTER              8 NOT NULL WITH DEFAULT
  5   WEIGHT        NUMERIC      3           NOT NULL WITH DEFAULT




                                                            BOTTOM

   F3=EXIT      F5=REFRESH      F12=CANCEL     F21=DISPLAY STATEMENT
```

Figure 5.5 Completed SPECIFY INSERT STATEMENT Second Screen

```
                    SPECIFY INSERT STATEMENT

   TYPE VALUES TO INSERT, PRESS ENTER.

      FIELD          VALUE
      PATIENT_ID     _
      FN
      LN
      PHONE
      WEIGHT









   F3=EXIT F5=REFRESH F6=INSERT LINE F10=COPY LINE F11=DISPLAY TYPE
   F12=CANCEL F14=DELETE LINE F15=SPLIT LINE F21=DISPLAY STATEMENT
```

Figure 5.6   SPECIFY INSERT STATEMENT Third Screen

```
                    SPECIFY INSERT STATEMENT

    TYPE VALUES TO INSERT, PRESS ENTER.

       FIELD          VALUE
       PATIENT_ID     '2050'
       FN             'Pete'
       LN             'Mark'
       PHONE          '555-1313'
       WEIGHT         180









   F3=EXIT F5=REFRESH F6=INSERT LINE F10=COPY LINE F11=DISPLAY TYPE
   F12=CANCEL F14=DELETE LINE F15=SPLIT LINE F21=DISPLAY STATEMENT
```

Figure 5.7   Completed SPECIFY INSERT STATEMENT Third Screen

```
        TOKEN Pete WAS NOT VALID. VALID TOKENS: + - ? :
          USER<FLOAT>
```

This error message occurs if you forget to place quotes around a value you are assigning to a CHAR type field. In this case, the first name of the patient (Pete) was typed erroneously as

```
                Pete
```

The correct entry would be

```
                'Pete'
```

BOO
BOO
BOX

THE UPDATE STATEMENT

The UPDATE statement is used to alter the values of specific columns that exist in a table or view. It is important to note that updating a value in a view also updates the value in the table upon which the view was based. Figure 5.8 illustrates the syntax of the UPDATE statement. Omitting the WHERE clause causes the change(s) specified in the SET clause to be applied to each row of the table. On the AS/400, up to 32,768 rows may be updated in any single UPDATE operation.*

```
UPDATE  |collection-name/table-name  |  SET  |column-name = expression, ... |
        |collection-name/view-name   |

 WHERE search-condition
```

Figure 5.8   Syntax Chart for UPDATE Statement

For example, to change the values in the HOSPITAL column to 'Fairfax' for *every* row in the SURGERY table, enter

```
        UPDATE MEDICAL/SURGERY
          SET HOSPITAL = 'Fairfax'
```

A specific row or rows may be identified for update by the WHERE clause. For example, to change the cost associated with the surgery whose identification number (SURGERY_ID) is 3000, enter

```
        UPDATE MEDICAL/SURGERY
          SET COST = 35000
          WHERE SURGERY_ID = '3000'
```

The UPDATE statement is not restricted to changing the value of only one column. The SET clause may introduce a list of column names and values. For example, to change the name of the hospital, the type of surgery, and the cost of the surgery whose identifica-

---

*If COMMIT (*NONE) is specified, any number of rows may be updated in a single UPDATE operation.

tion number is 3000, enter

```
UPDATE MEDICAL/SURGERY
    SET HOSPITAL = 'Hills', TYPE = 'Foot', COST = 5000
    WHERE SURGERY_ID = '3000'
```

In defining values for the column(s) in the SET clause, you may include expressions as well as a literal. For example, to raise the value associated with the cost for the surgery with the identification number 3000 by 10 percent, enter

```
UPDATE MEDICAL/SURGERY
    SET COST = COST * 1.1
    WHERE SURGERY_ID = '3000'
```

THE DELETE STATEMENT

The DELETE statement removes unwanted rows from a table. Note that deleting a row from a view also deletes the row from the table upon which the view was based. Figure 5.9 illustrates the syntax of the DELETE statement. The WHERE clause is optional. Including it restricts the deletion of rows to only those rows that meet the search condition.

```
DELETE FROM │collection-name/table-name │ ┌WHERE search-condition┐
            │collection-name/view-name  │ └                      ┘
```

Figure 5.9   Syntax Chart for DELETE Statement

For example, to delete only the data on surgeries that took place in Fairfax Hospital, enter

```
DELETE FROM MEDICAL/SURGERY
    WHERE HOSPITAL = 'Fairfax'
```

To delete *all* rows of a table, you would omit the WHERE clause. For example, if you wanted to delete all of the data in the SURGERY table, you would enter

```
DELETE FROM MEDICAL/SURGERY
```

Figure 5.10 illustrates the CONFIRM STATEMENT screen that results from a request to delete (or update) all of the data in a table. If you then pressed the Enter key, you would complete the process of deleting all of the records in the SURGERY table. Note that deleting all of the data in a table does *not* delete the table structure. You would use the DROP statement to delete the data *and* the structure.

> **TIP**   Remember that using DELETE without the WHERE clause will remove *all* your data. When you see a CONFIRM STATEMENT box, make sure you really want to perform the operation before answering.

```
                        CONFIRM STATEMENT

   YOU ARE ABOUT TO ALTER (DELETE OR UPDATE) ALL OF THE
   RECORDS IN YOUR FILE(S).

   PRESS ENTER TO CONFIRM YOUR STATEMENT TO ALTER THE ENTIRE
   FILE.

   PRESS F12=CANCEL TO RETURN AND CANCEL YOUR STATEMENT.




   F12=CANCEL
```

Figure 5.10   CONFIRM STATEMENT Screen

DATA FILE UTILITY (DFU)

The INSERT, UPDATE, and DELETE statements provide a useful, interactive method for inserting and maintaining data in a database. But many databases contain hundreds if not thousands of records. The INSERT statement is not usually used to load large quantities of data into a database. Instead, data entry or bulk load programs are usually coded and executed.

One method for loading large amounts of data into a database is to use a high-level language to create programs to do the loading. Another method is to use the AS/400's data file utility (DFU), which assists you in creating data entry/edit programs. DFU is an interactive utility for defining, creating, and maintaining programs used to add, change, delete, and display data in a database. Unlike high-level programming languages, DFU does not require extensive programming skills. Thus, the utility is a handy way to quickly develop and execute data entry and data maintenance programs.

To start the DFU utility, proceed to any AS/400 menu and at the command prompt enter the CL command

===>STRDFU

Figure 5.11 depicts the resulting AS/400 DATA FILE UTILITY (DFU) menu screen. The DFU menu offers five choices. You may choose to run an existing DFU program, create a new DFU program, change an existing DFU program, delete an existing DFU program, or quickly add data to a database file by creating and executing a temporary program. For further information on the DFU utility, press F1 (HELP) when the cursor is positioned on the AS/400 DATA FILE UTILITY (DFU) menu screen or refer to the *DFU User's Guide and Reference Manual.*

```
                    AS/400 DATA FILE UTILITY (DFU)

     SELECT ONE OF THE FOLLOWING:


          1. RUN A DFU PROGRAM
          2. CREATE A DFU PROGRAM
          3. CHANGE A DFU PROGRAM
          4. DELETE A DFU PROGRAM
          5. UPDATE DATA USING TEMPORARY PROGRAM






     SELECTION OR COMMAND
     ===>

     F3=EXIT    F4=PROMPT    F9=RETRIEVE    F12=CANCEL
```

Figure 5.11   AS/400 DATA FILE UTILITY (DFU) Menu Screen

SUMMARY

Data can be loaded into your physical data structures with the INSERT statement. Each INSERT statement entered will add one row of data into a table. Use of function key nine (F9) minimizes the amount of typing required to enter similar statements by retrieving the last statement entered. An alternative to typing the entire INSERT statement at the Interactive SQL prompt is to use the prompting feature (F4) of the AS/400.

The UPDATE statement is used to correct mistakes or revise data in a table. Updating a value in a view also updates the value in the table upon which the view was defined. On the AS/400, up to 32,768 rows may be updated in any single UPDATE operation.

The DELETE statement is used to remove either specific unwanted rows from a table or all rows. Note that deleting a row from a view also deletes the row from the table upon which the view was based.

The INSERT statement is one method for inserting data into a database, but it is not usually used to load large quantities of data. Instead, data entry or bulk load programs are usually coded and executed. The AS/400's data file utility (DFU) can be used to create the data entry/edit programs used to add, change, delete, and display data in a database.

QUESTIONS

1. What is the purpose of the INSERT statement? How is it used?
2. How can you use the INSERT statement to display on the screen a description of the structure of a table (i.e., what fields exist, the data types of the fields, and their length)?
3. When must a data value be enclosed in single quotation marks?
4. What does function key nine (F9) do?
5. What is the purpose of the UPDATE statement? How is it used?
6. How many rows may be updated in any single UPDATE operation?
7. What is the purpose of the DELETE statement? How is it used?
8. What is the difference between the DELETE statement and the DROP statement?
9. What is DFU?
10. How do you start DFU?

EXERCISES

1. Create, if you have not already, the example MEDICAL database depicted in Figure 4.2, and then use the INSERT statement to enter the data in Figure 5.1.
2. Use DFU to add the following PATIENT data to the database:

```
2450   Tim    Mary     555-2121   175
2500   Beth   George   555-2222   130
```

3. Use the DELETE statement to remove the data on Tim Mary from the MEDICAL database. Change the WEIGHT value to 120 for Beth George.
4. Use the DELETE statement to remove the data on Beth George from the MEDICAL database.

6

The AS/400 SELECT Statement

THE SELECT STATEMENT

The SELECT statement allows you to interactively query a database for information. Figure 6.1 outlines the syntax and form of the SELECT statement for Interactive SQL. The result of entering a SELECT statement is a table of information. This table of information

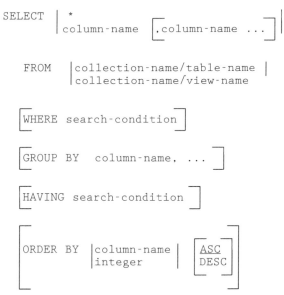

Figure 6.1 Syntax and Form of the SELECT Statement

is not permanent, and it does not alter the data or the structure of the database table(s) referenced to generate it.

For example, to display information on the patients in the database, proceed to the Interactive SQL screen (as described in Chapter 3) and enter

```
SELECT * FROM MEDICAL/PATIENT
```

The asterisk indicates that the resulting table should contain all of the columns in the PATIENT table. Figure 6.2 illustrates a resulting table of information. The information displayed is not in order by name or weight, but instead reflects the order in which the data were entered. The SELECT statement does not order the data unless the ORDER BY clause is used.

```
                              DISPLAY DATA
                                          DATA WIDTH ......: 49
      POSITION TO LINE ....._          SHIFT TO COLUMN ......
      ....+....1....+....2....+....3....+....4....+....5....
      PATIENT_ID   FN        LN            PHONE        WEIGHT
      2000         Joe       Dillon        555-1212     160
      2050         Pete      Mark          555-1313     180
      2100         Nancy     Smith         555-1414     120
      2150         Betty     Jones         555-1515     130
      2200         Frank     Lamb          555-1616     210
      2250         Mike      Post          555-1717     145
      2300         Sam       Parken        555-1818     220
      2350         Abby      Pearl         555-1919     105
      2400         Alice     Able          555-1010     160
      ******** END OF DATA ********



                                                   BOTTOM
      F3=EXIT  F12=CANCEL  F19=LEFT  F20=RIGHT  F21=SPLIT
```

Figure 6.2   Table Resulting from SELECT * FROM MEDICAL/PATIENT

CHOOSING PARTICULAR COLUMNS (FIELDS)

The asterisk used in the first example selected all columns; it may be replaced with a list of column names. Thus

```
SELECT PATIENT_ID, FN, LN, PHONE, WEIGHT FROM MEDICAL/PATIENT
```

is equivalent in results to SELECT * FROM MEDICAL/PATIENT, though it is more verbose.

Note: Copyrighted screens in this chapter are used by permission of IBM Corporation.

BOO BOO BOX	KEYWORD FROM NOT EXPECTED. VALID TOKENS: (+ - ? : USER
	The above error message is generated if you include an extra comma after the last column name, as in
	SELECT PATIENT_ID, FN, LN, PHONE, WEIGHT, FROM MEDICAL/PATIENT
	To correct the error in the above statement, remove the extra comma after the column name WEIGHT and reenter the statement.

BOO BOO BOX	TOKEN FN WAS NOT VALID. VALID TOKENS: , FROM INTO.
	The above error message is generated if you do not separate the column names with commas, as in
	SELECT PATIENT_ID FN LN PHONE WEIGHT FROM MEDICAL/PATIENT
	To correct the error, separate the column names with commas and reenter the statement.

The list of column names may consist of one or more column names. You do not have to include all of the column names that exist in the table that you are referencing. For example, you could enter

    SELECT LN FROM MEDICAL/PATIENT

to obtain a table of last names of patients.

You can also specify the column names in any order. For example,

    SELECT PHONE, LN, FN, FROM MEDICAL/PATIENT

is a valid statement that displays a table containing only the phone number, last name, and first name of patients.

THE WHERE CLAUSE

Just as you may choose particular columns in a query, you also may choose particular rows. The WHERE clause of the SELECT statement enables you to filter data so that only certain rows are displayed in the resulting table. For example, suppose we want information on the patient assigned the identification number 2100. Using the WHERE clause in the SELECT statement, we enter

    SELECT * FROM MEDICAL/PATIENT
    WHERE PATIENT_ID = '2100'

Since the PATIENT_ID column was defined as character type data, the patient identification number is enclosed in single quotes.

BOO BOO BOX

COMPARISON OPERATOR = OPERANDS NOT COMPATIBLE.

The above error message is generated if you omit the single quotes for a character type column, as in

```
SELECT * FROM MEDICAL/PATIENT
     WHERE PATIENT_ID = 2100
```

To correct the error, enclose the comparison value (the operand 2100) in single quotes (' ') and reenter the statement.

BOO BOO BOX

NAME "2100" NOT ALLOWED.

The above error message is generated if you use double quotes (" "). To correct the error, use single quote marks and reenter the statement.

If a column is defined as numeric, the comparison value must not be enclosed in quotes. For example, suppose we need to know which patients weigh over 200 pounds. We enter

```
SELECT * FROM MEDICAL/PATIENT
     WHERE WEIGHT > 200
```

In the previous two examples we have used two different comparison operators: the = (equal to) and the > (greater than) operators. The comparison operators that are available include

=	Equal to
< >	Not equal to
<	Less than
>	Greater than
>=	Greater than or equal to
<=	Less than or equal to

In addition to being used with comparison operators, the WHERE clause can be used with the logical operators AND, OR, and NOT. For example, to retrieve information on two types of surgeries, brain and heart, we use the logical operator OR and enter

```
SELECT * FROM MEDICAL/SURGERY
     WHERE TYPE = 'Brain' OR TYPE = 'Heart'
```

BOO
BOO
BOX

```
TOKEN <END-OF-STATEMENT> WAS NOT VALID. VALID TOKENS: <
```

The above error message is generated if you omit the column name in the latter half of the query, as in

```
SELECT * FROM MEDICAL/SURGERY
     WHERE TYPE = 'Brain' OR 'Heart'
```

To correct the error, edit the WHERE clause to include a complete expression after the OR conjunction:

```
SELECT * FROM MEDICAL/SURGERY
     WHERE TYPE = 'Brain' OR TYPE = 'Heart'
```

We could use the logical operator AND to display information on heart surgeries that were performed at Fairfax Hospital by entering

```
SELECT * FROM MEDICAL/SURGERY
     WHERE TYPE = 'Heart' AND HOSPITAL = 'Fairfax'
```

The logical operator NOT simply negates search criteria. For example, to display information on heart surgeries that were performed at hospitals other than Fairfax, we enter

```
SELECT * FROM MEDICAL/SURGERY
     WHERE TYPE = 'Heart' AND NOT (HOSPITAL = 'Fairfax')
```

Note that the parentheses are optional, but should be included for clarity.

In general, when search criteria are specified by a WHERE clause, each row of the named table is individually tested against the criteria. The row is included in the resulting table only if the result is *true* when the data items in that row are tested against the search criteria specified in the WHERE clause. Search criteria that include the logical operators will be interpreted according to the truth tables in Tables 6.1–6.3.

TABLE 6.1 TRUTH TABLE FOR AND OPERATOR

A	B	Result
True	True	True
True	False	False
False	True	False
False	False	False

TABLE 6.2 TRUTH TABLE FOR OR OPERATOR

A	B	Result
True	True	True
True	False	True
False	True	True
False	False	False

F16 — Main Menu

Or Go Main

F-3 Edit S&L

IN F10 Asst Options D2

Go DRBO

Ry. 9D

THANK YOU FOR ATTENDING THE LUCKY STORES, INC. JOB FAIR

September 7 & 8, 1995

Thank you for your interest in Lucky Stores, Inc. We appreciate the time you set aside to meet with us.

Because we have so many interested applicants, it will be impossible for us to respond to each of you. All applications will be reviewed to assess each applicant's qualifications and skills. If a second interview is appropriate, you will be called by September 19, 1995. Only those applicants who qualify for a second interview will be called.

So that we may process the extraordinary numbers of applications, we ask that you please do not call the Company or the Employment Development Department (EDD). While we appreciate your interest and enthusiasm, it will be nearly impossible to give you any feedback on your individual application.

Again, thank you very much and good luck in your job search.

TABLE 6.3 TRUTH TABLE
FOR NOT OPERATOR

A	Result
True	False
False	True

IN, BETWEEN, AND LIKE

The WHERE clause also supports the use of the predicates IN, BETWEEN, and LIKE. The IN predicate allows you to define a set of values that are acceptable. For example, our previous retrieval of information on brain and heart surgeries could have been accomplished by entering

```
SELECT * FROM MEDICAL/SURGERY
    WHERE TYPE IN ('Brain', 'Heart')
```

instead of

```
SELECT * FROM MEDICAL/SURGERY
    WHERE TYPE = 'Brain' OR TYPE = 'Heart'
```

The BETWEEN predicate defines a range of acceptable values, which includes the values specified as the beginning and end parameters. For example, to find out which patients weigh from 150 to 200 pounds, we enter

```
SELECT * FROM MEDICAL/PATIENT
    WHERE WEIGHT BETWEEN 150 AND 200
```

The LIKE predicate provides for pattern recognition within character data. Using the LIKE predicate and its supported wildcards, we can specify a character or series of characters to be compared to the data contained in a particular column. For example, to retrieve information on all patients whose last name begins with the letter P, we enter

```
SELECT * FROM MEDICAL/PATIENT
    WHERE LN LIKE 'P%'
```

There are two wildcard characters available for use with the LIKE predicate: the percent sign (%) and the underscore (_). The percent sign is used to represent zero, one, or more characters. In the previous example, we said that as long as the last name began with the letter P, we didn't care what characters (or number of characters) followed.

The underscore wildcard character is used to specify a particular character location. Consider the following statement:

```
SELECT * FROM MEDICAL/PATIENT
   WHERE FN LIKE '_e%'
```

The underscore indicates that the first letter in the first name field is insignificant. The percent sign indicates that whatever follows the letter "e" is insignificant. Basically, we are looking for anyone whose first name includes the letter "e" in the second position.

THE ORDER BY CLAUSE

In Chapter 1 we noted that one of the definitive characteristics of a relational database table is that the order of the rows within the table is considered arbitrary. The table that appears on the screen as a result of executing the statement SELECT * FROM MEDICAL/PATIENT illustrates how data are not ordered. The rows in the resulting table are not arranged by name or weight, but instead reflect the order in which the data were entered. The ORDER BY clause provides a mechanism for presenting the rows of the resulting table in a particular order.

For example, to display information on patients sorted by last name, enter

```
SELECT * FROM MEDICAL/PATIENT
   ORDER BY LN
```

Ordering of rows may be specified as either ascending (ASC) or descending (DESC). Ascending is the default. For example, to display information on patients sorted by last name in descending order (from Z to A), enter

```
SELECT * FROM MEDICAL/PATIENT
   ORDER BY LN DESC
```

Rows also may be ordered on multiple fields. For example, to display information on patients sorted by first and last name in descending order (from Z to A), enter

```
SELECT * FROM MEDICAL/PATIENT
   ORDER BY LN DESC, FN DESC
```

Up to 10,000 columns* may be specified in an ORDER BY clause.[1]

SUMMARY

The Interactive SQL SELECT statement allows you to interactively query the database for information. The result of entering a SELECT statement is a temporary table of information, which does not alter the data or the structure of the database table(s) referenced to generate it.

---

*Early versions of the AS/400 system provided for only 256 columns or 256 bytes to be specified in an ORDER BY clause and for only 120 columns or 120 bytes if the ORDER BY clause contained columns defined as floating point columns.[2]

The SELECT statement allows you to choose particular columns in a query. The WHERE clause of the SELECT statement enables you to filter data so that only certain rows are displayed in the resulting table. The WHERE clause also supports the use of the predicates IN, BETWEEN, and LIKE.

The IN predicate allows you to define a set of acceptable values. The BETWEEN predicate allows you to define an inclusive range of acceptable values. The LIKE predicate provides for pattern recognition within character data. Through the use of the LIKE predicate and its supported wildcards, you can specify a character or series of characters to be compared to the data contained in a particular column. The ORDER BY clause puts the rows of the resulting table in a specified order.

ENDNOTES

1. *Application System/400 Systems Application Architecture Structured Query Language/400 Reference (SC41-9608-03), Version 2*, IBM Corporation, 4th ed. (November 1993), p. 285.
2. *Application System/400 Programming: Structured Query Language/400 Reference (SC21-9608-2)*, IBM Corporation, 3rd ed. (August 1990), p. 62.

QUESTIONS

1. Why might SQL's SELECT statement be considered the basis of a DBMS query language?
2. How does the SQL SELECT statement compare to the relational SELECT operator discussed in Chapter 1?
3. What effect(s) does the execution of a SELECT statement have on the contents and/or structure of the referenced table?
4. What does an asterisk immediately following the SELECT statement verb indicate?
5. When must a comparison value in a SELECT statement be enclosed in quotes?
6. What purpose does the WHERE clause serve?
7. What comparison operators are available to form an expression that is a part of an SQL statement?
8. What logical operators are available to form an expression that is a part of an SQL statement?
9. How is the IN predicate similar to the OR operator?
10. What purpose does the ORDER BY clause serve?

EXERCISES

1. This practice exercise requires the completion of Exercise 1 in Chapter 5. Sign on to the AS/400, start an Interactive SQL session, and execute the appropriate SELECT statement to
   a. List the names of patients in descending alphabetical order.
   b. List the names of only those surgeries with a name beginning with the letter 'H'.

   c. List data on only those surgeries with a cost exceeding $10,000.

   d. Display data on the doctor whose phone number is 555-5555.

   e. Display data on those surgeries that were performed at Fairfax Hospital and had a cost exceeding $30,000.

2. Contrast the use of the SELECT statement on the AS/400 with the use of retrieval commands/techniques provided with personal computer DBMS packages such as dBASE.*

---

*dBASE is a registered trademark of Ashton-Tate Corporation.

7

Using AS/400 SQL Functions

AS/400 SQL FUNCTIONS DEFINED

The ability to query a database for information is enhanced by the AS/400 SQL functions. A function is an operation that returns a single value based on the evaluation of one or more operands provided. Syntactically, functions substitute for column names in a SELECT statement and are expressed as the function name followed by one or more operands enclosed in parentheses. For example, in the statement

```
SELECT MAX(WEIGHT)
    FROM MEDICAL/PATIENT
```

the function is MAX, which returns the maximum value in a set of values, and the operand is the column name WEIGHT. The displayed result of this query will be the weight of the heaviest patient.

BOO BOO BOX	COLUMN SPECIFIED IN SELECT LIST NOT VALID.
	
	The above error message is generated if you mix column names and column functions, as in
	
	`SELECT LN, MAX(WEIGHT)`
	`    FROM MEDICAL/PATIENT`
	
	If the SELECT statement does not include a GROUP BY or HAVING clause (discussed in Chapter 8), column names and column functions cannot both be in the same statement.

The *IBM Application System/400 Systems Application Architecture Structured Query Language/400 Reference* defines a function as

> An operation denoted by a function name followed by one or more operands which are enclosed in parentheses. The operands of functions are called arguments. Most functions have a single argument that is specified by an expression. The result of a function is a single value derived by applying the function to the result of the expression.[1]

There are two types of functions: column and scalar. A column function accepts an argument that references a set of values. The reference manual states, "The values of the argument are specified by an expression. This expression must include at least one column-name and must not include a column function."[2]

The AS/400 SQL column functions include

AVG	Returns the average of a set of numbers.
COUNT	Returns the number of rows or values in a set of rows or values.
MAX	Returns the maximum value in a set of values.
MIN	Returns the minimum value in a set of values.
STDDEV	Returns the standard deviation of a set of numbers.
SUM	Returns the sum of a set of numbers.
VAR	Returns the variance of a set of numbers.

A scalar function accepts an argument that references a single value. The reference manual states, "The restrictions on the use of column functions do not apply to scalar functions because a scalar function is applied to a single value rather than a set of values."[3] The AS/400 SQL scalar functions include

ABSVAL	Returns the absolute value of a number.
ACOS	Returns the arc cosine of a number, in radians.
ANTILOG	Returns the antilogarithm (base 10) of a number.
ASIN	Returns the arc sine of a number, in radians.
ATAN	Returns the arc tangent of a number, in radians.
ATANH	Returns the hyperbolic arc tangent of a number, in radians.
CHAR	Returns a string representation of date/time value.
COS	Returns the cosine of a number.
COSH	Returns the hyperbolic cosine of a number.
COT	Returns the cotangent of a number.
DATE	Returns a date from a value.
DAY	Returns the day part of a value.
DAYS	Returns an integer representation of a date.

DECIMAL	Returns a packed decimal representation of a numeric value.
DIGITS	Returns a character string representation of a number.
EXP	Returns a value that is the base of the natural logarithm *(e)* raised to a power specified by the argument.
FLOAT	Returns a floating point representation of a number.
HEX	Returns a hexidecimal representation (string of hexadecimal digits) of a value.
HOUR	Returns the hour part of a value.
INTEGER	Returns an integer representation of a number.
LAND	Returns a string that is the logical AND of the argument strings.
LENGTH	Returns the length of a value.
LN	Returns the natural logarithm of a number.
LOG	Returns the common logarithm (base 10) of a number.
LOR	Returns a string that is the logical OR of the argument strings.
LNOT	Returns a string that is the logical NOT of the argument string.
MAX	Returns the maximum value in a set of values.
MICROSECOND	Returns the microsecond part of a value.
MIN	Returns the minimum value in a set of values.
MINUTE	Returns the minute part of a value.
MOD	Returns the remainder of the division of the first argument by the second argument.
MONTH	Returns the month part of a value.
SECOND	Returns the seconds part of a value.
SIN	Returns the sine of a number.
SINH	Returns the hyperbolic sine of a number.
SQRT	Returns the square root of a number.
STRIP	Removes blanks or another specified character from the end or beginning of a string expression.
SUBSTR	Returns a substring of a string.
TAN	Returns the tangent of a number.
TANH	Returns the hyperbolic tangent of a number.
TIME	Returns a time from a value.
TIMESTAMP	Returns a timestamp from a value or pair of values.
TRANSLATE	Translates the SBCS characters of the argument to uppercase.
VALUE	Returns the first argument that is not null.
XOR	Returns a string that is the logical XOR of the argument strings.
YEAR	Returns the year part of a value.
ZONED	Returns a zoned decimal representation of a number.

THE AVG FUNCTION

The AVG function is a column function that provides the average of a collection of numbers. For example, to find the average cost of surgeries performed at Fairfax Hospital, enter

```
SELECT AVG(COST)
    FROM MEDICAL/SURGERY
    WHERE HOSPITAL = 'Fairfax'
```

The argument values of the function (in our example, the database entries for the column COST) must be numeric, and their sum must be within the range of the data type of the result.[4]

THE COUNT FUNCTION

The COUNT function is a column function that provides a count of the number of rows in a database table or the number of values in a particular row. For example, to determine how many patients are in the MEDICAL database (assuming each row is a unique patient), enter the statement

```
SELECT COUNT(*)
    FROM MEDICAL/PATIENT
```

The asterisk argument instructs the system to count all rows in the named table. Duplicate rows and null-valued rows are included in the count.

BOO BOO BOX	TOKEN PATIENT_ID WAS NOT VALID. VALID TOKENS: *.
	
	 The above error message occurs if the asterisk is replaced with the field name PATIENT_ID, as in
	
	 `SELECT COUNT(PATIENT_ID)`
	 `    FROM MEDICAL/PATIENT`
	
	 Unlike some versions of SQL, Interactive SQL on the AS/400 does not permit an alternative use of the COUNT function.

THE MAX FUNCTION

The MAX function is a column function that reports the maximum value within a set of values. For example, to determine the cost of the most expensive surgery in the MEDICAL database, enter the statement

```
SELECT MAX(COST)
    FROM MEDICAL/SURGERY
```

The argument values of the function (in our example, the database entries for the column COST) can be any values except character strings that have a maximum length greater than 256. If the function is applied to an empty set, the result is a null value. Otherwise, the result is the maximum value in the set.[5]

THE MIN FUNCTION

The MIN function is a column function that reports the minimum value within a set of values. For example, to determine the lightest patient weight in the MEDICAL database, enter

```
SELECT MIN(WEIGHT)
     FROM MEDICAL/PATIENT
```

The argument values of the function (in our example, the database entries for the column WEIGHT) can be any values other than character strings whose maximum lengths are greater than 256. If the function is applied to an empty set, the result is a null value. Otherwise, the result is the minimum value in the set.[6]

THE SUM FUNCTION

The SUM function is a column function that provides the sum of a collection of numbers. For example, to find the total cost of surgeries performed at Fairfax Hospital, enter

```
SELECT SUM(COST)
     FROM MEDICAL/SURGERY
     WHERE HOSPITAL = 'Fairfax'
```

The argument values of the function (in our example, the database entries for the column COST) must be numeric, and their sum must be within the range of the data type of the result.[7]

THE DECIMAL FUNCTION

Consider the statement

```
SELECT AVG(WEIGHT)
     FROM MEDICAL/PATIENT
```

This query returns the average weight of the patients in the database. The answer displayed is

```
158.8888888888888888888888888888
```

Although this answer is correct, for business applications a more reasonable answer might be simply 158 or 158.88. The DECIMAL function limits, or strips away, the long tail of 8s. Specifically, the DECIMAL function is a scalar function that produces a packed decimal representation of a numeric value. For example,

```
SELECT DECIMAL(AVG(WEIGHT), 4, 0)
     FROM MEDICAL/PATIENT
```

yields the simplified answer 158. A simple modification to the function parameters,

```
SELECT DECIMAL(AVG(WEIGHT), 5, 2)
     FROM MEDICAL/PATIENT
```

yields the answer 158.88.

The general format of the DECIMAL function is

$$DECIMAL(expression \left[, \; integer \left[, \; integer\right]\right])$$

where the evaluation of the expression must result in a number. The expression may optionally be followed by an integer value that specifies the precision to which the resulting number will be displayed. The second integer in the format specifies the scale (the number of digits to the right of the decimal point) to which the resulting number will be displayed and also is optional.

The first integer, if specified, must fall in the range of 1 to 31. If the first integer is not specified, the default number depends on the data type of the expression as follows:

15 for floating point, numeric, or nonzero scale binary

11 for large integer

5 for small integer

The second integer, if specified, must be in the range from zero to whatever was specified for the first integer. If the second integer is not specified, the default is a specification of zero.[8]

	++++++
	The above response indicates that the answer cannot be expressed to the given precision and scale, as in
BOO BOO BOX	`SELECT DECIMAL(AVG(WEIGHT), 4, 2)` `     FROM MEDICAL/PATIENT`
	Be sure to specify a precision that allows for the scale you desire. In the example, to achieve a scale of 2, change the 4 to a 5:
	`SELECT DECIMAL(AVG(WEIGHT), 5, 2)` `     FROM MEDICAL/PATIENT`

THE DIGITS FUNCTION

The DIGITS function is a scalar function that produces a character string representation of a number. For example, it might take the form

```
SELECT *
   FROM MEDICAL/PATIENT
   WHERE DIGITS(WEIGHT) = '160'
```

The general format of the DIGITS function is

```
DIGITS(expression)
```

where the evaluation of the expression must result in a numeric value. The result of executing the function is a fixed-length string of digits that represents the absolute value of the expression, without regard to its scale. The result is not signed, nor does it include a decimal point. The result includes leading zeroes as necessary to ensure that the length of the resulting string is five positions if the expression is a small zero-scale integer, ten positions if the expression is a large zero-scale integer, or a number of positions equal to the precision of the expression value if the expression is a decimal, numeric, or nonzero-scale integer with defined precision.[9]

THE FLOAT FUNCTION

The FLOAT function is a scalar function that produces a floating point representation of a number. For example,

```
SELECT FLOAT(COST)
   FROM MEDICAL/SURGERY
```

results in

```
2.500000000000000E+004
5.000000000000000E+003
4.500098000000000E+004
2.750050000000000E+004
7.000450000000000E+003
3.650980000000000E+003
3.500576000000000E+004
```

The general format of the function is

```
FLOAT(expression)
```

where the evaluation of the expression must result in a numeric value. The result of executing the function is a double-precision floating point number. The result is the same number that would occur if the expression were assigned to a double-precision floating point column or variable.[10]

THE INTEGER FUNCTION

The INTEGER function is a scalar function that produces an integer representation of a number. For example,

```
SELECT INTEGER(AVG(COST))
   FROM MEDICAL/SURGERY
```

yields

$$21,165$$

as opposed to

$$21,165.5242857142857142857142857 1$$

which is the result of using the AVG function without the INTEGER function, as in

```
SELECT AVG(COST)
  FROM MEDICAL/SURGERY
```

The general format of the function is

```
INTEGER(expression)
```

where the evaluation of the expression must result in a numeric value. The result of executing the function is a large integer with zero scale. The result is the same number that would occur if the expression were assigned to a large integer column or variable.[11]

THE LENGTH FUNCTION

The LENGTH function is a scalar function that provides the length of a particular value, such as a column. For example,

```
SELECT LENGTH(FN)
  FROM MEDICAL/PATIENT
```

yields

```
LENGTH ( FN )
     10
     10
     10
     10
     10
     10
     10
     10
     10
```

The general format of the function is

```
LENGTH(expression)
```

where the expression can be any value. The result of executing the function is a large integer with zero scale that specifies the number of bytes used to represent the expression value. In our example, it gave the number of bytes required to store a first name (the FN column). The value returned depends on the data type. For character strings, the resulting number is the length of the string, including blanks; for small integers, it is a value of 2; for large integers and single-precision floating point numbers, it is a value of 4; and for double-precision floating point numbers, it is a value of 8.[12] The LENGTH function provides a quick way to determine how much space a field uses.

THE SUBSTR FUNCTION

The SUBSTR function is a scalar function that produces a substring of a string. For example, to list the names of patients whose last name begins with the letter P, enter

```
SELECT *
    FROM MEDICAL/PATIENT
    WHERE SUBSTR(LN, 1, 1) = 'P'
```

The general format of the function is

$$SUBSTR(expression, \ integer \ \boxed{, \ integer} \ )$$

where the expression must be a string expression. The first integer specifies the starting location (the first character of the resulting string). The integer specifying the starting position must be between 1 and the length of the string. The second integer is optional and specifies the length of the resulting string. If specified, the length must be an integer between 1 and n, where n is the length attribute of the specified string minus the starting position (the first integer) plus 1. If the second integer is not specified, the default is the length of the string minus the integer specified as the starting value plus 1.[13]

SUMMARY

The AS/400 SQL functions enhance the user's ability to query a database for information. A function is an operation that returns a single value based on the evaluation of one or more operands. Syntactically, functions substitute for column names in the SELECT statement and are denoted by a function name followed by the operand(s) enclosed in parentheses.

There are two types of functions: column and scalar. The AS/400 SQL column functions include AVG, COUNT, MAX, MIN, STDDEV, SUM, and VAR. The AS/400 SQL scalar functions include ABSVAL, ACOS, ANTILOG, ASIN, ATAN, ATANH, CHAR, COS, COSH, COT, DATE, DAY, DAYS, DECIMAL, DIGITS, EXP, FLOAT, HEX, HOUR, INTEGER, LAND, LENGTH, LN, LOG, LOR, LNOT, MAX, MICROSECOND, MIN, MINUTE, MOD, MONTH, SECOND, SIN, SINH, SQRT, STRIP, SUBSTR, TAN, TANH, TIME, TIMESTAMP, TRANSLATE, VALUE, XOR, YEAR, and ZONED.

ENDNOTES

1. *Application System/400 Systems Application Architecture Structured Query Language/400 Reference (SC41-9608-03), Version 2*, IBM Corporation, 4th ed. (November 1993), p. 81.
2. Ibid.
3. Ibid., p. 89.
4. Ibid., p. 82.
5. Ibid., p. 84.

6. Ibid., p. 85.
7. Ibid., p. 87.
8. Ibid., p. 104.
9. Ibid., p. 105.
10. Ibid., p. 107.
11. Ibid., p. 110.
12. Ibid., p. 112.
13. Ibid., p. 131.

QUESTIONS

1. What purpose do functions serve?
2. Name the column functions.
3. Name the scalar functions.
4. Compare column functions and scalar functions. What distinguishes a column function from a scalar function?
5. What does the system message + + + + + + indicate in reference to the execution of a function?

EXERCISES

1. This exercise requires the completion of Exercise 1 in Chapter 5. In an Interactive SQL session, enter the appropriate SELECT statement to
   a. Display the name of the heaviest patient.
   b. Display data on the least expensive surgery.
   c. Display the average cost, to the second decimal point, of surgery performed at Fairfax Hospital.
   d. Use the SUBSTR function to list the names of patients whose first name begins with the letter A.
   e. Display the length of the HOSPITAL column using the LENGTH function.
2. Contrast the use of the LIKE predicate with the use of the SUBSTR function in a SELECT command. Give examples of statements showing their similarities and differences.

8

More AS/400 SELECT Power

Chapter 6 introduced the SELECT statement as the basis for performing queries. In this chapter we will examine two clauses used in the SELECT statement, the GROUP BY clause and the HAVING clause, and discuss getting information from multiple tables. We will also examine the AS/400 prompting feature that alters the SELECT statement to a fill-in-the-blanks request for information.

THE GROUP BY CLAUSE

It was noted in Chapter 7 that column names and column functions cannot be specified in the same SELECT statement. However, by using the GROUP BY clause it is possible to include column names and column functions in the same SELECT statement. The GROUP BY clause logically collects rows based on common values within a particular column. Column functions (AVG, COUNT, MAX, MIN, STDDEV, SUM, VAR) may be applied to these logical collections. For example, to find the sum of the costs of surgeries performed at each of the various hospitals, enter

```
SELECT HOSPITAL, SUM(COST)
    FROM MEDICAL/SURGERY
    GROUP BY HOSPITAL
```

Figure 8.1 illustrates the result of such a query on the sample database.

```
                            DISPLAY DATA
                                          DATA WIDTH ......: 59
POSITION TO LINE ....._            SHIFT TO COLUMN ......
....+....1....+....2....+....3....+....4....+....5....+....
HOSPITAL                                          SUM (COST)
Arlington                                          50,657.19
Fairfax                                            97,501.48
******** END OF DATA ********




                                                        BOTTOM
 F3=EXIT   F12=CANCEL   F19=LEFT   F20=RIGHT   F21=SPLIT
```

Figure 8.1   Table Resulting from SELECT HOSPITAL, SUM(COST)
FROM MEDICAL/SURGERY
GROUP BY HOSPITAL

THE HAVING CLAUSE

The HAVING clause applies a search condition based on column function(s) to a logical collection of rows derived as a result of a GROUP BY clause. For example, to find the sum of the costs of surgeries performed at each of the various hospitals at which four or more surgeries were performed, enter

```
SELECT HOSPITAL, SUM(COST)
    FROM MEDICAL/SURGERY
    GROUP BY HOSPITAL
    HAVING COUNT(*) > 3
```

Since only Arlington had more than three surgeries, this statement would display the sum of costs of surgeries performed there.

Note: Copyrighted screens in this chapter are used by permission of IBM Corporation.

MULTIPLE TABLES QUERY

A key concept of the relational database approach is that relationships are carried in the data. In the MEDICAL database in Figure 8.2, the patient identification number (PATIENT_ID) appears as a column in three separate tables: PATIENT, SURGERY, and DOCPAT. The PATIENT_ID in the PATIENT table provides access to descriptive data on a patient, but provides no data on what surgeries a patient has undergone. In the SURGERY table, the PATIENT_ID identifies the patient who had surgery, but yields no descriptive data on the patient.

The relationship of patient to surgeries (1:N) is established by carrying the patient identification number (PATIENT_ID) within the SURGERY table. The relationship of patients to doctors (N:M) is established by maintaining a table that consists only of patient and doctor identification numbers. This intersection of PATIENT_ID and DOCTOR_ID is found in the DOCPAT table.

But if information is separated, how do we retrieve information on surgeries that patients have undergone, along with descriptive data on the patients? The task is to logi-

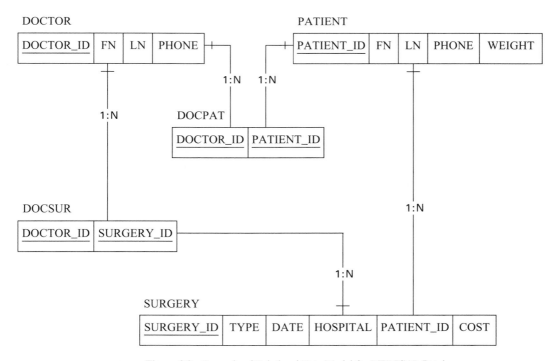

Figure 8.2   Example of Relational Data Model for MEDICAL Database

cally join the two tables together, as Figure 8.3 illustrates. In order for two tables to be joined, there must be a common column that exists in both. The PATIENT_ID occurs in both the PATIENT table and the SURGERY table. The following statement yields both information on surgeries that patients have undergone and descriptive data on the patients:

```
SELECT PATIENT.FN, PATIENT.LN, PATIENT.PHONE, SURGERY.TYPE,
      SURGERY.DATE, SURGERY.HOSPITAL, SURGERY.COST
   FROM MEDICAL/PATIENT, MEDICAL/SURGERY
   WHERE PATIENT.PATIENT_ID = SURGERY.PATIENT_ID
```

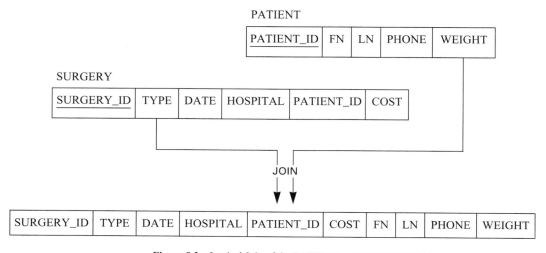

Figure 8.3   Logical Join of the PATIENT and SURGERY Tables

Each field name is prefixed with the name of the table of which it is a member. (Note the use of a period to separate the table name from the column name.) Assigning an alias to a table name conserves space and reduces the typing burden. Thus, the previous statement may be entered as

```
SELECT P.FN, P.LN, P.PHONE, S.TYPE, S.DATE, S.HOSPITAL, S.COST
   FROM MEDICAL/PATIENT P, MEDICAL/SURGERY S
   WHERE P.PATIENT_ID = S.PATIENT_ID
```

SELECT WITHIN A SELECT

Another way to join two tables in a query is to place a SELECT statement within a SELECT statement. For example, to determine which patients have had surgeries costing more than $25,000, enter

```
SELECT FN, LN
   FROM MEDICAL/PATIENT
   WHERE PATIENT_ID IN (SELECT PATIENT_ID FROM MEDICAL/SURGERY
                          WHERE COST > 25000)
```

The SELECT within parentheses references the SURGERY table and produces a group of patient identification numbers (PATIENT_IDs) for patients who have had surgeries costing more than $25,000. The search criteria of the first SELECT use this information to retrieve the corresponding names of the patients.

PROMPT (F4) SELECT

An alternative to typing the entire SELECT statement and then entering it at the Interactive SQL prompt is to use the prompting feature (F4) of the AS/400. The prompting feature (F4) reduces the query procedure to a fill-in-the-blanks request for information.

To demonstrate, let's reenter the statement to find the sum of the costs of surgeries performed at each of the various hospitals at which four or more surgeries were performed. The SELECT statement that was previously entered at the Interactive SQL prompt was

```
SELECT HOSPITAL, SUM(COST)
    FROM MEDICAL/SURGERY
    GROUP BY HOSPITAL
    HAVING COUNT(*) > 3
```

To reenter the statement using the prompting feature of the AS/400, type the word SELECT and then press function key four (F4), instead of pressing the Enter key.

BOO BOO BOX	TOKEN <END-OF-STATEMENT> WAS NOT VALID. VALID TOKENS: Pressing the Enter key instead of F4 will yield the above error message. To correct the error, simply press the F4 key, *not* the Enter key.

The SPECIFY SELECT STATEMENT screen illustrated in Figure 8.4 will be displayed. The flashing cursor prompts you to name the table (file) from which you wish to select data. The message on the line above the cursor instructs you to type the desired information for the SELECT statement. The message also informs you that you may press the F4 key and let the system provide you with a list of names. To work our example, type the valid name MEDICAL/SURGERY and then press the Return key (*not* the Enter key).

TIP   Use the Return key to move from field to field. Press the Enter key only after you have typed entries for all screen items.

Complete the SPECIFY SELECT STATEMENT screen as depicted in Figure 8.5 and then press the Enter key. The response of the system will be the same display table that was generated by entering the entire SELECT statement at the Interactive SQL prompt.

```
                         SPECIFY SELECT STATEMENT

        TYPE INFORMATION FOR SELECT STATEMENT.  PRESS F4 FOR A LIST.

            FROM FILES..............._
            SELECT FIELDS...........
            WHERE CONDITIONS........
            GROUP BY FIELDS.........
            HAVING CONDITIONS.......
            ORDER BY FIELDS.........
            FOR UPDATE OF FIELDS....

                                                                BOTTOM
        TYPE CHOICES, PRESS ENTER.

            NUMBER OF RECORDS TO OPTIMIZE..........
            DISTINCT RECORDS IN RESULT FILE........   N   Y=YES, N=NO
            FOR FETCH ONLY........................   N   Y=YES, N=NO
            UNION WITH ANOTHER SELECT.............   N   Y=YES, N=NO

        F3=EXIT F4=PROMPT F5=REFRESH F6=INSERT LINE F9=SPECIFY SUBQRY
        F10=COPY LINE F12=CANCEL F14=DEL LINE F15=SPLIT LINE F24=MORE
```

Figure 8.4   SPECIFY SELECT STATEMENT Screen

```
                         SPECIFY SELECT STATEMENT

        TYPE INFORMATION FOR SELECT STATEMENT.  PRESS F4 FOR A LIST.

            FROM FILES............. medical/surgery
            SELECT FIELDS........... hospital,sum(cost)
            WHERE CONDITIONS........
            GROUP BY FIELDS......... hospital
            HAVING CONDITIONS....... count(*) > 3
            ORDER BY FIELDS.........
            FOR UPDATE OF FIELDS....

                                                                BOTTOM
        TYPE CHOICES, PRESS ENTER.

            NUMBER OF RECORDS TO OPTIMIZE..........
            DISTINCT RECORDS IN RESULT FILE........   N   Y=YES, N=NO
            FOR FETCH ONLY........................   N   Y=YES, N=NO
            UNION WITH ANOTHER SELECT.............   N   Y=YES, N=NO

        F3=EXIT F4=PROMPT F5=REFRESH F6=INSERT LINE F9=SPECIFY SUBQRY
        F10=COPY LINE F12=CANCEL F14=DEL LINE F15=SPLIT LINE F24=MORE
```

Figure 8.5   Completed SPECIFY SELECT STATEMENT Screen

> **T I P**   To learn more about each of the options that are a part of the SPECIFY
> SELECT STATEMENT screen, move the cursor to the appropriate line and press
> F1 (the help key).

SUMMARY

The GROUP BY clause logically collects rows based on common values within a particular column. Column functions (AVG, COUNT, MAX, MIN, STDDEV, SUM, VAR)
may be applied to these logical collections. The HAVING clause applies a search condition based on column function(s) to a logical collection of rows derived from a GROUP
BY clause.

The SELECT statement can be used with multiple tables if they have a common column. By referencing multiple tables and including a SELECT statement within a SELECT
statement, you can extend the query capabilities of Interactive SQL. The AS/400 prompting
feature (F4) reduces the SELECT statement to a fill-in-the-blanks request for information.

QUESTIONS

1. Why might you use the GROUP BY clause?
2. Why might you use the HAVING clause?
3. How can multiple tables be joined in a display table? What restrictions are there?
4. How is a SELECT within a SELECT similar to a join operation?
5. What function key supports the prompting feature of the AS/400?

EXERCISE

1. This exercise requires the completion of Exercise 1 in Chapter 5. In an Interactive SQL session,
   a. Enter each of the sample statements discussed in this chapter.
   b. Use the SELECT statement to display a table of information that includes patient names
      and the names of the patients' doctors.

9

Query/400

DEFINING QUERY/400

Query/400 is a menu-driven, decision support utility that helps you select, arrange, and report data stored in one or more AS/400 database files. Unlike the Interactive SQL SELECT statement, Query/400 is capable of generating reasonably sophisticated query reports. Column spacing, numeric editing, and providing control breaks (for points where the column values change) are some of the features Query/400 provides that the SELECT statement does not.

To execute a query (and thus generate a report) using Query/400, you first define the form of the query. Simply stated, you create a template that specifies how you wish the data to be presented. You detail such things as which database file(s) to reference and how you want the reported information to appear (descriptive column names, calculated values, numeric editing, summary functions, page breaks, etc.).

When you execute (run) a query, you direct the system to generate a report based on the template you have built. In Query/400 terms, a template is called a *query definition*. A query definition may be executed, saved, modified, and/or deleted.

> ### DEFINITION
> In Query/400 terms, a **query definition** is information stored in the system that describes a query.[1] You may reference a query definition to execute it (run the query), modify it, or delete it from storage on the system.

HOW TO ACCESS QUERY/400

After signing on to the AS/400 system, you may access the Query/400 utility by

1. going to the DECISION SUPPORT menu and choosing the QUERY/400 utility option or
2. entering the CL command STRQRY (or another appropriate CL command—see the section on Query/400 Menu Options) at the command prompt that is presented at the bottom of any AS/400 menu screen.

Traversing Menus to Access Query/400

There are two ways to reach the DECISION SUPPORT menu, where QUERY/400 is an option. The first is to traverse through the menus. From the MAIN MENU depicted in Figure 9.1, choose the second option (OFFICE TASKS) by entering a "2" at the command prompt.

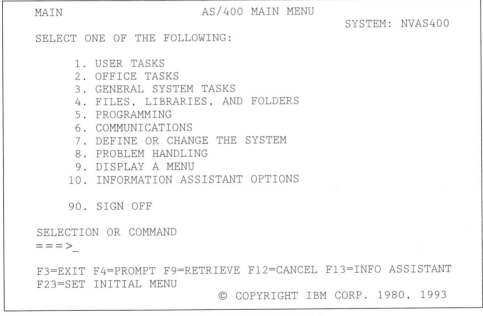

```
    MAIN                        AS/400 MAIN MENU
                                                   SYSTEM: NVAS400
    SELECT ONE OF THE FOLLOWING:

          1. USER TASKS
          2. OFFICE TASKS
          3. GENERAL SYSTEM TASKS
          4. FILES, LIBRARIES, AND FOLDERS
          5. PROGRAMMING
          6. COMMUNICATIONS
          7. DEFINE OR CHANGE THE SYSTEM
          8. PROBLEM HANDLING
          9. DISPLAY A MENU
         10. INFORMATION ASSISTANT OPTIONS

         90. SIGN OFF

    SELECTION OR COMMAND
    ===>_

    F3=EXIT F4=PROMPT F9=RETRIEVE F12=CANCEL F13=INFO ASSISTANT
    F23=SET INITIAL MENU
                            © COPYRIGHT IBM CORP. 1980, 1993
```

Figure 9.1   The AS/400 MAIN MENU Screen

The system will respond with the OFFICE TASKS menu depicted in Figure 9.2. From the OFFICE TASKS menu, choose the third option (DECISION SUPPORT) by entering a "3" at the command prompt.

Note: Copyrighted screens in this chapter are used by permission of IBM Corporation.

```
OFCTSK                       OFFICE TASKS
                                            SYSTEM: NVAS400
SELECT ONE OF THE FOLLOWING:

      1. AS/400 OFFICE - OFFICEVISION/400
      2. HOST SYSTEM TASKS FOR AS/400 PC SUPPORT
      3. DECISION SUPPORT
      4. OFFICE SECURITY
      5. DISPLAY SYSTEM DIRECTORY
      6. WORK WITH SYSTEM DIRECTORY
      7. DOCUMENTS
      8. FOLDERS

     70. RELATED COMMANDS



SELECTION OR COMMAND
===>_

F3=EXIT F4=PROMPT F9=RETRIEVE F12=CANCEL F13=INFO ASSISTANT
F16=AS/400 MAIN MENU
                        © COPYRIGHT IBM CORP. 1980, 1993
```

Figure 9.2   The AS/400 OFFICE TASKS Menu Screen

```
DECISION                  DECISION SUPPORT
                                            SYSTEM: NVAS400
SELECT ONE OF THE FOLLOWING:

      1. INTERACTIVE DATA DEFINITION UTILITY (IDDU)
      2. QUERY UTILITIES
      3. BUSINESS GRAPHICS UTILITY (BGU)
      4. INTERACTIVE SQL

     20. FILES


     70. RELATED COMMANDS



SELECTION OR COMMAND
===>_

F3=EXIT F4=PROMPT F9=RETRIEVE F12=CANCEL F13=INFO ASSISTANT
F16=AS/400 MAIN MENU
                        © COPYRIGHT IBM CORP. 1980, 1993
```

Figure 9.3   The AS/400 DECISION SUPPORT Menu Screen

```
QUERY                    QUERY UTILITIES

SELECT ONE OF THE FOLLOWING:

  QUERY/400
     1. WORK WITH QUERIES
     2. RUN AN EXISTING QUERY
     3. DELETE A QUERY

  SQL/400
    10. START SQL/400 QUERY MANAGER

  QUERY MANAGEMENT
    20. WORK WITH QUERY MANAGEMENT FORMS
    21. WORK WITH QUERY MANAGEMENT QUERIES
    22. START A QUERY
    23. ANALYZE A QUERY/400 DEFINITION
                                              MORE...
SELECTION OR COMMAND
= = = >_

F3=EXIT F4=PROMPT F9=RETRIEVE F12=CANCEL F13=INFO ASSISTANT
F16=AS/400 MAIN MENU
```

Figure 9.4   The QUERY UTILITIES Menu First Screen

```
QUERY                    QUERY UTILITIES

SELECT ONE OF THE FOLLOWING:

    24. START A QUERY ALLOWING QUERY/400 DEFINITIONS

  RELATED MENUS
    30. FILES
    31. OFFICE TASKS




                                              BOTTOM
SELECTION OR COMMAND
= = = >_

F3=EXIT F4=PROMPT F9=RETRIEVE F12=CANCEL F13=INFO ASSISTANT
F16=AS/400 MAIN MENU
```

Figure 9.5   The QUERY UTILITIES Menu Second Screen

The system will respond with the DECISION SUPPORT menu depicted in Figure 9.3. From the DECISION SUPPORT menu, choose the second option (QUERY UTILITIES) by entering a "2" at the command prompt.

The system will respond with the QUERY UTILITIES menu screen depicted in Figure 9.4. Note the message "MORE. . ." on the bottom right of the screen. This message informs us that there is an additional screen to the QUERY UTILITIES menu.

Press the F8 key to page forward and see the second part of the QUERY UTILITIES menu, depicted in Figure 9.5. Note the message "BOTTOM" on the bottom right of the screen. This message informs us that there are no additional screens that are a part of the QUERY UTILITIES menu. Press the F7 key to page backward and return to the first half of the QUERY UTILITIES menu.

Menu Shortcut

A second way to traverse menus is to use the GO command. Entering the GO command along with the name of the desired menu causes the system to jump directly to that menu. Thus, if you enter

```
===>GO QUERY
```

at the command prompt, the system will jump directly to the QUERY UTILITIES menu depicted in Figure 9.4.

The STRQRY Command

The fastest way to gain access to the Query/400 utility is to enter the STRQRY command at the command prompt

```
===>STRQRY
```

The system will go directly to the QUERY UTILITIES menu screen depicted in Figure 9.4.

BOO BOO BOX	COMMAND STARTQRY IN LIBRARY *LIBL NOT FOUND. If you misspell the STRQRY command, you will receive an error message similar to the one above. In this case the command was erroneously spelled STARTQRY. No harm has been done. To correct the error, simply type the command correctly at the command prompt and press the Enter key.

QUERY/400 FUNCTION KEYS

Note that the list of defined function keys on the bottom of the QUERY UTILITIES menu screen depicted in Figure 9.4 includes F3, F4, F9, F12, F13, and F16. The definition of these function keys, as well as of some others that are not displayed on the screen but are nonetheless available for your use, follows:

F1=HELP	Provides information on using the system. The information displayed depends on where you are when you request help. Help is context-sensitive, which means that the information provided is related to the ongoing action.
F3=EXIT	Exits from the current Query/400 menu and returns to the menu from which it was started.
F4=PROMPT	Provides assistance in entering or selecting a command.
F7=SCROLL BACKWARD	Returns to the previous screen. When working with multiple screens of information, you will see the note "MORE. . ." or "BOTTOM" on the bottom right side of the screen. As you read through the multiple screens, use this function key to get back to the previous screen.
F8=SCROLL FORWARD	Advances to the following screen. When working with multiple screens of information, you will see the note "MORE. . ." on the bottom right side of the screen. Use this function key to go on to the next screen of information.
F9=RETRIEVE	Retrieves a previously entered CL command.
F12=CANCEL	Cancels the current display or command and returns to the previous display.
F13=INFORMATION ASSISTANT (USER SUPPORT on early versions)	Displays the Information Assistant options (displays the SESSION SERVICES menu on early versions of AS/400 system).
F16=AS/400 MAIN MENU	Returns to the AS/400 MAIN MENU screen.

QUERY/400 MENU OPTIONS

The QUERY UTILITIES menu, illustrated in Figures 9.4 and 9.5, offers four categories that collectively feature eleven options. The four categories (QUERY/400, SQL/400, QUERY MANAGEMENT, and RELATED MENUS) provide services to define queries, run queries, produce formatted reports, and access menus that offer related services such as access to DFU and Interactive SQL.

Each option on the QUERY UTILITIES menu has a corresponding CL command that may be entered at any AS/400 command prompt, thus saving you the trouble of traversing through a series of menu screens. The menu options and their corresponding CL commands are listed in Table 9.1.

TABLE 9.1   CL COMMANDS FOR MENU OPTIONS

Menu Option	CL Command
1. WORK WITH QUERIES	WRKQRY
2. RUN AN EXISTING QUERY	RUNQRY
3. DELETE A QUERY	DLTQRY
10. START SQL/400 QUERY MANAGER	STRQM
20. WORK WITH QUERY MANAGEMENT FORMS	WRKQMFORM
21. WORK WITH QUERY MANAGEMENT QUERIES	WRKQMQRY
22. START A QUERY	STRQMQRY
23. ANALYZE A QUERY/400 DEFINITION	ANZQRY
24. START A QUERY ALLOWING QUERY/400 DEFINITIONS	STRQMQRY
30. FILES	GO FILE
31. OFFICE TASKS	GO OFCTSK

The focus of our discussion will be on the three options offered within the menu category QUERY/400. These options are WORK WITH QUERIES, RUN AN EXISTING QUERY, and DELETE A QUERY. The option WORK WITH QUERIES is used to create, maintain, display, and execute a query definition. The option RUN AN EXISTING QUERY is used to execute an existing query. The option DELETE A QUERY is used to remove a query definition from the system.

WORK WITH QUERIES Option

The first option on the QUERY UTILITIES menu, WORK WITH QUERIES, is the starting point for using Query/400. You select this option by entering "1" at the command prompt or by entering the CL command WRKQRY at the command prompt on any AS/400 menu screen. Either way, the system will respond with the WORK WITH QUERIES screen shown in Figure 9.6.

As depicted in Figure 9.6, you are asked to select one of several different tasks and to identify the query definition that you wish to use. If you specify a query name, the system will search the library specified. If you are creating a new query, the system will store the completed query definition in the named library under the query name you enter.

As an example, we will use the WORK WITH QUERIES option to create a query definition on surgeries performed (using the data in our MEDICAL database created in previous chapters). Figure 9.7 illustrates naming the query MEDRPT and storing it in a library called NVHOVEJ (be sure to name a library to which you have access).

Press the Enter key, and the DEFINE THE QUERY screen, shown in Figure 9.8, will be displayed. The DEFINE THE QUERY screen offers eleven different query definition options. The first option (SPECIFY FILE SELECTIONS) is the only option you are

```
                         WORK WITH QUERIES

TYPE CHOICES, PRESS ENTER.

   OPTION . . . . . .   1        1=CREATE,2=CHANGE,3=COPY,4=DELETE
                                 5=DISPLAY, 6=PRINT DEFINITION
                                 8=RUN IN BATCH, 9=RUN
   QUERY . . . . . .             NAME, F4 FOR LIST
      LIBRARY . . . . xxxxxxx    NAME,*LIBL,F4 FOR LIST










   F3=EXIT         F4=PROMPT        F5=REFRESH        F12=CANCEL
                                 © COPYRIGHT IBM CORP. 1988
```

Figure 9.6   The WORK WITH QUERIES Screen

```
                         WORK WITH QUERIES

TYPE CHOICES, PRESS ENTER.

   OPTION . . . . . .   1        1=CREATE,2=CHANGE,3=COPY,4=DELETE
                                 5=DISPLAY, 6=PRINT DEFINITION
                                 8=RUN IN BATCH, 9=RUN
   QUERY . . . . . .   medrpt    NAME, F4 FOR LIST
      LIBRARY . . . . nvhovej    NAME,*LIBL,F4 FOR LIST










   F3=EXIT         F4=PROMPT        F5=REFRESH        F12=CANCEL
                                 © COPYRIGHT IBM CORP. 1988
```

Figure 9.7   Sample of Completed WORK WITH QUERIES Screen

required to select. You may select one or more (or all) of the options to define your query. To select an option, just type "1" next to the desired option. Each option you select will invoke a separate process after you press the Enter key. Each process will include one or more subsequent screen displays. Table 9.2 provides a brief description of each of the eleven options you may select in defining your query.

TABLE 9.2   DEFINE THE QUERY OPTIONS

Option	Use
SPECIFY FILE SELECTIONS	Required; declares the file(s) on which to base the query.
DEFINE RESULT FIELDS	Defines fields that hold the result of a calculation based on existing fields.
SELECT AND SEQUENCE FIELDS	Selects and orders the fields of the report.
SELECT RECORDS	Includes only certain records in the report.
SELECT SORT FIELDS	Identifies fields used to sort the output.
SELECT COLLATING SEQUENCE	Identifies a collating sequence, such as EBCDIC.
SPECIFY REPORT COLUMN FORMATTING	Specifies column headings, spacing, and other formats for fields in the report.
SELECT REPORT SUMMARY FUNCTIONS	Specifies summary functions such as total, average, and count.
DEFINE REPORT BREAKS	Specifies how records should be grouped in the report.
SELECT OUTPUT TYPE AND OUTPUT FORM	Selects the output medium of the report (paper, screen, or file).
SPECIFY PROCESSING OPTIONS	Specifies special processing options such as ignoring decimal data errors and truncating or rounding decimal output.

Source: Application System/400 Query/400 User's Guide (SC41-9614-00), Version 2, IBM Corporation, 1st ed. (May 1991), pp. 3-3 and 3-4.

TIP   Press the Tab key or the Return key to move down a line to select additional query definition options. If you press the Enter key, the system will process what you have typed and move on to the next screen in the query definition process.

In Figure 9.9, the SPECIFY FILE SELECTIONS and SPECIFY REPORT COL- UMN FORMATTING options are selected. To continue our example, type a "1" next to each of these options and then press the Enter key. The next screen displayed will be the SPECIFY FILE SELECTIONS screen, shown in Figure 9.10. This screen is used to name the database file or files that are to be queried for information.

Figure 9.11 shows the completed screen for our example. Enter SURGERY as the (table) file name to be referenced for our query. Then press the Tab key to move to the next line to specify the library in which to store our query definition. Rather than using the default library name, type in the library (collection) name MEDICAL and press the Enter key. The system will respond with the message

SELECT FILE(S), OR PRESS ENTER TO CONFIRM.

```
                      DEFINE THE QUERY

QUERY . . . . . . :  MEDRPT    OPTION . . . . . :  CREATE
  LIBRARY . . . . :  NVHOVEJ   CCSID . . . . . :  65535

TYPE OPTIONS, PRESS ENTER.  PRESS F21 TO SELECT ALL.
  1=SELECT


OPT    QUERY DEFINITION OPTION
 1     SPECIFY FILE SELECTIONS
       DEFINE RESULT FIELDS
       SELECT AND SEQUENCE FIELDS
       SELECT RECORDS
       SELECT SORT FIELDS
       SELECT COLLATING SEQUENCE
       SPECIFY REPORT COLUMN FORMATTING
       SELECT REPORT SUMMARY FUNCTIONS
       DEFINE REPORT BREAKS
       SELECT OUTPUT TYPE AND OUTPUT FORM
       SPECIFY PROCESSING OPTIONS


F3=EXIT        F5=REPORT        F12=CANCEL
F13=LAYOUT     F18=FILES        F21=SELECT ALL
```

Figure 9.8 The DEFINE THE QUERY Screen

```
                      DEFINE THE QUERY

QUERY . . . . . . :  MEDRPT    OPTION . . . . . :  CREATE
  LIBRARY . . . . :  NVHOVEJ   CCSID . . . . . :  65535

TYPE OPTIONS, PRESS ENTER.  PRESS F21 TO SELECT ALL.
  1=SELECT


OPT    QUERY DEFINITION OPTION
 1     SPECIFY FILE SELECTIONS
       DEFINE RESULT FIELDS
       SELECT AND SEQUENCE FIELDS
       SELECT RECORDS
       SELECT SORT FIELDS
       SELECT COLLATING SEQUENCE
 1     SPECIFY REPORT COLUMN FORMATTING
       SELECT REPORT SUMMARY FUNCTIONS
       DEFINE REPORT BREAKS
       SELECT OUTPUT TYPE AND OUTPUT FORM
       SPECIFY PROCESSING OPTIONS


F3=EXIT        F5=REPORT        F12=CANCEL
F13=LAYOUT     F18=FILES        F21=SELECT ALL
```

Figure 9.9 Sample of Completed DEFINE THE QUERY Screen

```
                    SPECIFY FILE SELECTIONS

TYPE CHOICES, PRESS ENTER.  PRESS F9 TO SPECIFY AN ADDITIONAL
   FILE SELECTION.

   FILE . . . . . . . . .                NAME, F4 FOR LIST
      LIBRARY . . . . . .  NVHOVEJ       NAME, *LIBL, F4 FOR LIST
   MEMBER . . . . . . . . *FIRST         NAME, *FIRST, F4 FOR LIST
   FORMAT . . . . . . . . *FIRST         NAME, *FIRST, F4 FOR LIST




   F3=EXIT       F4=PROMPT       F5=REPORT        F9=ADD FILE
   F12=CANCEL    F13=LAYOUT      F24=MORE KEYS
```

Figure 9.10 The SPECIFY FILE SELECTIONS Screen

```
                    SPECIFY FILE SELECTIONS

TYPE CHOICES, PRESS ENTER.  PRESS F9 TO SPECIFY AN ADDITIONAL
   FILE SELECTION.

   FILE . . . . . . . . .  surgery      NAME, F4 FOR LIST
      LIBRARY . . . . . .  medical      NAME, *LIBL, F4 FOR LIST
   MEMBER . . . . . . . . *FIRST        NAME, *FIRST, F4 FOR LIST
   FORMAT . . . . . . . . *FIRST        NAME, *FIRST, F4 FOR LIST




   F3=EXIT       F4=PROMPT       F5=REPORT        F9=ADD FILE
   F12=CANCEL    F13=LAYOUT      F24=MORE KEYS
```

Figure 9.11 Completed SPECIFY FILE SELECTIONS Screen

at the bottom of the display screen. Although you could now select another file, in order to use more than one database file and join tables, this example references only a single file. Press the Enter key to conclude work with the option SPECIFY FILE SELECTIONS. The system will present the SPECIFY REPORT COLUMN FORMATTING screen illustrated in Figure 9.12, because this was the second option we selected when we defined our query (see Figure 9.9).

```
                    SPECIFY REPORT COLUMN FORMATTING

     TYPE INFORMATION, PRESS ENTER.
       COLUMN HEADINGS:   *NONE, ALIGNED TEXT LINES

                    COLUMN
     FIELD          SPACING    COLUMN HEADING       LEN    DEC     EDIT
     SURGERY_ID        0       SURGERY_ID            4



     TYPE              2       TYPE                 10



     DATE              2       DATE                 10



                                                            MORE...

     F3=EXIT        F5=REPORT    F10=PROCESS/PREVIOUS      F12=CANCEL
     F13=LAYOUT     F16=EDIT     F18=FILES           F23=LONG COMMENT
```

Figure 9.12   The SPECIFY REPORT COLUMN FORMATTING Screen

The SPECIFY REPORT COLUMN FORMATTING screen allows you to specify the number of spaces between columns, the column headings, and the size of columns. The field names, column headings, and column lengths shown in Figure 9.12 are taken from the definitions of the SURGERY file in the MEDICAL database file.

The COLUMN SPACING column specifies the number of spaces that should be displayed to the left of the named field (column). Note that the default is to place no spaces to the left of the first field and two spaces between all subsequent fields. If you would like to adjust the number of spaces between fields in your query report, you simply type over the default number in the COLUMN SPACING column.

The length (LEN) and decimal (DEC) columns specify the width of the column and the number of decimal positions to be shown for numeric data displayed in the column. Specifying a length or decimal value does not change the actual length or decimal value of the data—it only affects how the data are displayed in the query report. If you specify a length of zero, the field will be omitted from the query report. The EDIT column is used to specify a format for the display of numeric fields.

To continue our example, we will use the SPECIFY REPORT COLUMN FOR-
MATTING screen to enter more descriptive column names for the query report, otherwise
accepting the defaults (see Figure 9.13). Note the message "MORE. . ." on the bottom of
the screen. By pressing F8, you can page forward to a screen that has the remaining fields
of our query. After you have finished specifying how you wish the query report to be formatted, press the Enter key. The DEFINE THE QUERY screen will be displayed. As illustrated in Figure 9.14, the completed options are marked with a greater than sign (>).

To conclude the definition of the query report, press F3. The system will display the
EXIT THIS QUERY screen shown in Figure 9.15. Make sure that the name of the query
is MEDRPT and that it is saved in a library of your choice (NVHOVEJ in this example).
Respond yes (Y) to save the definition.

In saving a definition, you can use the TEXT prompt to enter a comment of up to 50
characters, describing your query. This comment would then be displayed whenever the
list of queries was displayed. The AUTHORITY prompt is used to indicate what kind of
access other users may have to your query definition. Continuing our example, select
option 1 (to run interactively) and press the Enter key. The results of the query report are
featured in Figure 9.16.

```
                    SPECIFY REPORT COLUMN FORMATTING

     TYPE INFORMATION, PRESS ENTER.
        COLUMN HEADINGS:   *NONE, ALIGNED TEXT LINES

                     COLUMN
     FIELD           SPACING    COLUMN HEADING      LEN    DEC    EDIT
     SURGERY_ID        0        SURGERY_ID           4



     TYPE              2        SURGERY TYPE        10



     DATE              2        DATE OF SURGERY     10



                                                            MORE...

     F3=EXIT         F5=REPORT      F10=PROCESS/PREVIOUS       F12=CANCEL
     F13=LAYOUT      F16=EDIT       F18=FILES            F23=LONG COMMENT
```

Figure 9.13 Sample Completed SPECIFY REPORT COLUMN FORMATTING Screen

```
                       DEFINE THE QUERY

 QUERY . . . . . . :   MEDRPT     OPTION . . . . .:   CREATE
   LIBRARY . . . . :   NVHOVEJ    CCSID . . . . .:    65535

 TYPE OPTIONS, PRESS ENTER.  PRESS F21 TO SELECT ALL.
   1=SELECT

 OPT    QUERY DEFINITION OPTION
     >  SPECIFY FILE SELECTIONS
        DEFINE RESULT FIELDS
        SELECT AND SEQUENCE FIELDS
        SELECT RECORDS
        SELECT SORT FIELDS
        SELECT COLLATING SEQUENCE
     >  SPECIFY REPORT COLUMN FORMATTING
        SELECT REPORT SUMMARY FUNCTIONS
        DEFINE REPORT BREAKS
        SELECT OUTPUT TYPE AND OUTPUT FORM
        SPECIFY PROCESSING OPTIONS


 F3=EXIT          F5=REPORT        F12=CANCEL
 F13=LAYOUT       F18=FILES        F21=SELECT ALL
```

Figure 9.14   The DEFINE THE QUERY Screen with Selected Options Marked

```
                       EXIT THIS QUERY

 TYPE CHOICES, PRESS ENTER.

   SAVE DEFINITION . . .  Y            Y=YES, N=NO

   RUN OPTION  . . . . .  1            1=RUN INTERACTIVELY
                                       2=RUN IN BATCH
                                       3=DO NOT RUN

   FOR A SAVED DEFINITION:
     QUERY . . . . . . .  MEDRPT       NAME
       LIBRARY . . . . .  NVHOVEJ      NAME, F4 FOR LIST

     TEXT  . . . . . .  .

     AUTHORITY . . . . .  *LIBCRTAUT   *LIBCRTAUT, *CHANGE, *ALL,
                                       *EXCLUDE, *USE
                                       AUTHORIZATION LIST NAME



 F4=PROMPT     F5=REPORT      F12=CANCEL        F13=LAYOUT
 F14=DEFINE THE QUERY
```

Figure 9.15   The EXIT THIS QUERY Screen

```
                          DISPLAY REPORT

    QUERY . . . :   NVHOVEJ/MEDRPT          REPORT WIDTH . . . :   88
    POSITION TO LINE . . . .                SHIFT TO COLUMN . . . .
    LINE     ....+....1....+....2....+....3....+....4....+....5....
            SURGERY ID   SURGERY TYPE   DATE OF SURGERY HOSPITAL
    000001    3000       Heart           10/10/92       Fairfax
    000002    3010       Cosmetic        12/31/91       Arlington
    000003    3100       Brain           11/09/92       Fairfax
    000004    3150       Heart           11/30/92       Fairfax
    000005    3200       Hernia          10/16/92       Arlington
    000006    3250       Cosmetic        10/12/92       Arlington
    000007    3300       Heart           11/02/91       Arlington
    * * * * * *  * * * * * * * *   END OF REPORT * * * * * * * * *




                                                              BOTTOM

    F3=EXIT      F12=CANCEL      F19=LEFT      F20=RIGHT      F21=SPLIT
```

Figure 9.16 The DISPLAY REPORT Screen

RUN AN EXISTING QUERY Option

After you have created and saved a query definition, you may execute the query, without redefining it, by selecting the RUN AN EXISTING QUERY option from the QUERY UTILITIES menu depicted in Figure 9.4. From the QUERY UTILITIES menu, choose the second option by entering "2" at the command prompt. The system will respond with the RUN QUERY (RUNQRY) screen depicted in Figure 9.17. If we specify MEDRPT as the query and NVHOVEJ (for our example) as the library, the same report we created previously will be displayed, as illustrated in Figure 9.16.

As the title of the RUN QUERY (RUNQRY) screen suggests, an alternative way to execute (run) a query is to enter the CL command RUNQRY followed by the name of the query at the command prompt on the bottom of any AS/400 menu screen. For example, we might enter

===>RUNQRY MEDRPT

BOO BOO BOX	QUERY NAME OR FILE NAME MUST BE SPECIFIED.
	This error message will be displayed on the bottom of the screen if you neglect to specify the name of the query definition you wish to run. The RUNQRY command must be followed by the name of a query definition. Our example uses the MEDRPT query definition we created in the previous section.

```
                      RUN QUERY  (RUNQRY)

 TYPE CHOICES,  PRESS ENTER.

 QUERY  .  .  .  .  .  .  .  .     MEDRPT      NAME,  *NONE
    LIBRARY  .  .  .  .  .  .  .   NVHOVEJ     NAME,  *LIBL,  *CURLIB
 QUERY FILE:
    FILE  .  .  .  .  .  .  .  .               NAME,  *SAME
       LIBRARY  .  .  .  .  .  .      *LIBL    NAME,  *RUNOPT,  *LIBL,  *CURLIB
    MEMBER  .  .  .  .  .  .  .      *FIRST    NAME,  *RUNOPT,  *FIRST,  *LAST
          + FOR MORE VALUES
 REPORT OUTPUT TYPE  .  .        *RUNOPT    *RUNOPT,  *DISPLAY ...
 OUTPUT FORM  .  .  .  .  .  .    *RUNOPT    *RUNOPT,  *DETAIL,  *SUMMARY
 RECORD SELECTION   .  .  .      *NO        *NO,  *YES




                                                            BOTTOM

 F3=EXIT   F4=PROMPT   F5=REFRESH   F12=CANCEL   F13=HOW TO USE
 F24=MORE KEYS                                  THIS DISPLAY
```

Figure 9.17   The RUN QUERY (RUNQRY) Screen

DELETE A QUERY Option

To delete a query definition from storage on the system, you select the DELETE A QUERY option from the QUERY UTILITIES menu depicted in Figure 9.4. From the QUERY UTILITIES menu, choose the third option by entering "3" at the command prompt. The system will respond with the DELETE QUERY (DLTQRY) screen depicted in Figure 9.18. As the title of the screen suggests, an alternative way to reach the DELETE QUERY (DLTQRY) screen is to enter the CL command DLTQRY at the command prompt on the bottom of any AS/400 menu screen:

===>DLTQRY

In the DELETE QUERY screen, if you were to specify MEDRPT as the query and NVHOVEJ (for this example) as the library and then press the Enter key, the system would respond by deleting the query definition. The system would then return to the QUERY UTILITIES menu and display on the bottom of the screen a message such as

```
OBJECT MEDRPT IN NVHOVEJ TYPE *QRYDFN DELETED.
```

```
                        DELETE QUERY (DLTQRY)

TYPE CHOICES, PRESS ENTER.

QUERY . . . . . . . . .              NAME, *NONE
  LIBRARY . . . . . . .    *LIBL    NAME, *LIBL, *CURLIB




                                                            BOTTOM

F3=EXIT   F4=PROMPT   F5=REFRESH   F12=CANCEL   F13=HOW TO USE
F24=MORE KEYS                                    THIS DISPLAY
```

Figure 9.18   The DELETE QUERY (DLTQRY) Screen

TIP   Unlike the RUNQRY command, the DLTQRY command may be entered with or without the name of the query definition (query name or file name) to be deleted. If you enter the DLTQRY command without specifying a query definition, you are presented with the DELETE QUERY (DLTQRY) screen. If you enter the DLTQRY command and specify a query definition, as in

====>DLTQRY MEDRPT

the system does not display the DELETE QUERY (DLTQRY) screen, but simply deletes the query definition and displays a message informing you of the deletion.

SUMMARY

Query/400 is a menu-driven decision support utility that helps you select, arrange, and report on the data stored in one or more AS/400 database files. Query/400 provides more services than the Interactive SQL SELECT command; it can generate formatted reports that may include numeric editing and control breaks.

Query/400 reports on data stored in a database file based on a query definition. You may reference a query definition to execute it, modify its definition, or delete it from storage on the system.

The Query/400 utility may be started by choosing it as an option from the DECISION SUPPORT menu or by entering the CL command STRQRY. Other CL commands are also available to support access to the services of Query/400.

The QUERY UTILITIES menu offers a menu category called QUERY/400, which, in turn, offers three options. The option WORK WITH QUERIES is used to create, maintain, display, and execute a query definition. The option RUN AN EXISTING QUERY is used to execute an existing query. The option DELETE A QUERY is used to remove a query definition from the system.

ENDNOTE

1. *Application System/400 Query Management/400 Programmer's Guide and Reference (SC41-0090-01), Version 2*, IBM Corporation, 2nd ed. (November 1993), p. G-4.

QUESTIONS

1. What is Query/400?
2. What is query definition?
3. How does using Query/400 compare to using the Interactive SQL SELECT statement?
4. How do you access Query/400?
5. Which AS/400 menu has QUERY UTILITIES as an option?
6. How might you access Query/400 using AS/400 CL commands?
7. What are the three options of Query/400 listed on the QUERY UTILITIES menu? What services do they provide?
8. How do you define and execute a query using Query/400 without saving a query definition?
9. Using Query/400, how do you execute a query that was defined and saved previously?
10. Using Query/400, how do you delete a query definition?

EXERCISES

1. Locate a terminal or work station that has access to an AS/400. Sign on to the AS/400 system. Begin with the AS/400 main menu and traverse through the menus, ultimately selecting the option to start Query/400. Exit Query/400. Use the STRQRY command to start a Query/400 session. Exit Query/400. Use the WRKQRY command to work with Query/400. Contrast the various approaches.

2. Sign on to your AS/400 system, access Query/400, and work through each of the examples provided in this chapter.

3. Create a query definition to report on the patients in the MEDICAL database discussed in previous chapters. Run the query. Modify the query (for example, delete a field in the report or add extra spaces between columns). Run the modified query. Delete the query.

10

A Practice Exercise

In this chapter we will review and practice what we have discussed in the previous chapters. During the course of this exercise we will use Interactive SQL on AS/400 to

create a database
query the database, and
maintain the data in the database.

Figure 10.1 is a relational data model that depicts a typical academic environment. The model includes tables to store data on courses (COURSE) that are attended by students (STUDENT) and taught by teachers (TEACHER). Data are also kept on the grades (GRADE) earned by students and on where students live (HOUSING).

Relationships between the tables are indicated in the diagram. For example, the line labeled 1:N between the STUDENT relation and the GRADE relation illustrates the fact that a student may attend many courses. The table TCOURSE is an intersection table which provides for the fact that a teacher may teach many courses and that a course may be taught by more than one teacher (an N:M relationship between teacher and course).

Our exercise will involve logging on to the AS/400, creating the database, working with the database, and logging off the system.

THE SIGN-ON PROCESS

Starting a work session on the AS/400 requires establishing communication between your work station and the AS/400. This process is referred to as the sign-on process.

114

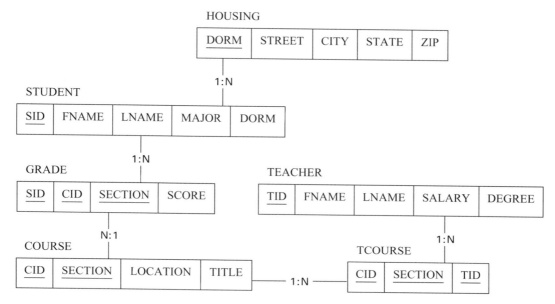

Figure 10.1   Relational Data Model for a SCHOOL Database

The sign-on process will vary from one site to another. The process described here is that followed by the Computing Center at Northern Virginia Community College (NVCC), Annandale, Virginia. Although access procedures may differ, generally the menu screens generated by the AS/400 will be the same. Consult your system administrator or instructor to resolve any differences.

The first step in accessing the AS/400 is to obtain a user ID and a password from your instructor or system administrator. Next, locate a terminal or PC that can connect to the AS/400.

Figure 10.2 depicts the initial screen you will probably see. This is not an AS/400 screen, but rather a screen used to provide access to the various systems available. To access the AS/400 system from this screen, you would enter the command "AS400" at the command prompt located near the bottom of the screen.

D E F I N I T I O N

The phrase **enter a command** means to type the desired command and then press the Enter key. Please note that the Enter key and the Return key do not have the same effect, unlike these keys on a personal computer. The Enter key signals the system to process what has been typed. The Return key (often symbolized by an arrow bent to the left) simply moves the cursor down a line. The Backspace key or arrow keys may be used to correct a typing error before the Enter key is pressed.

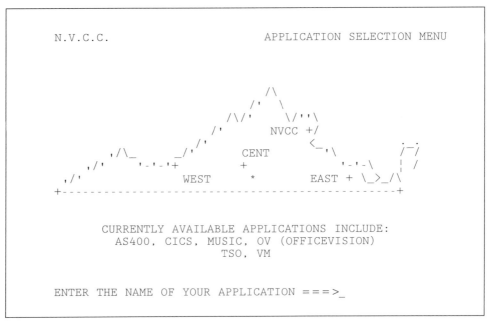

Figure 10.2   Initial Entry Screen to Access AS/400

Figure 10.3 depicts the resulting sign-on screen. Type your user ID, press the Return key (the bent arrow), type your password (the password is not displayed as you type it), and then press the Enter key.

BOO BOO BOX	CPF 1107 - PASSWORD NOT CORRECT FOR USER PROFILE Do not press the Enter key until you have typed both your user ID and your password. The Enter key signals the system to process what you have typed. If you type your user ID and then press the Enter key, the system will respond with the above error message. To correct the problem, press the Return key (Tab key on the PC), type your password, and then press the Enter key. The Return key does not signal the system to process an entry, but instead simply moves the cursor down a line.

The first time you sign on to the NVCC AS/400 computer, you are asked to change your password. See Appendix C for a discussion of changing your password.

With the exception of the request to change your password (or to alter a user profile, a topic beyond the scope of this book), the AS/400 MAIN MENU screen is the first screen presented upon entry into the system. Figure 10.4 illustrates the AS/400 MAIN MENU screen.

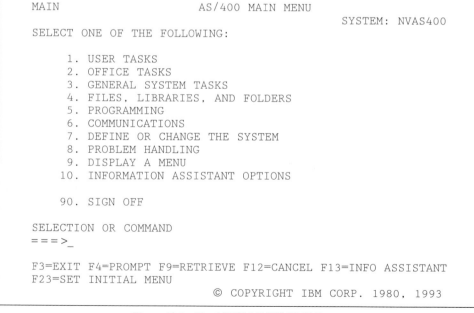

```
                              SIGN ON


        NN      NN VV    VV CCCCC  CCCCC      SYSTEM.....: NVAS400
        NNN    NN VV    VV CCCCC  CCCCC      SUBSYSTEM..:  QINTER
        NNNN   NN VV   VV CC      CC         DISPLAY....:  NVHCF4
      NN NNNN   VV   VV CC      CC
      NN   NNN   VV VV   CCCCC  CCCCC
     NN    NN    VVV     CCCCC  CCCCC


        AA     SSSSSSS      ///    44   44   00000     00000
       AA AA   S            ///    44    44  00   00   00   00
       AA   AA  SSSSS       ///    44444444  00    00  00    00
      AAAAAAA        S  ///         44  00    00  00    00
     AA     AA       S  ///         44  00   00   00   00
     AA     AA  SSSSSSS  ///        44   00000     00000


                 USERID  ................  _
                 PASSWORD ..............


     ENTER USERID AND PASSWORD OR LEAVE FIELD BLANK FOR DEMO AND
     HIT ENTER
```

Figure 10.3   AS/400 NVCC Sign-On Screen

```
    MAIN                      AS/400 MAIN MENU
                                                    SYSTEM: NVAS400
    SELECT ONE OF THE FOLLOWING:

         1. USER TASKS
         2. OFFICE TASKS
         3. GENERAL SYSTEM TASKS
         4. FILES, LIBRARIES, AND FOLDERS
         5. PROGRAMMING
         6. COMMUNICATIONS
         7. DEFINE OR CHANGE THE SYSTEM
         8. PROBLEM HANDLING
         9. DISPLAY A MENU
        10. INFORMATION ASSISTANT OPTIONS

        90. SIGN OFF

    SELECTION OR COMMAND
    ===>_

    F3=EXIT F4=PROMPT F9=RETRIEVE F12=CANCEL F13=INFO ASSISTANT
    F23=SET INITIAL MENU
                        © COPYRIGHT IBM CORP. 1980, 1993
```

Figure 10.4   The AS/400 MAIN MENU Screen

Note: Copyrighted screens in this chapter are used by permission of IBM Corporation.

After signing on to the AS/400 system, you can start an Interactive SQL session by entering the STRSQL command at the command prompt:

===>STRSQL

The system will respond with the Interactive SQL screen depicted in Figure 10.5. SQL statements may now be entered.

```
                           ENTER SQL STATEMENTS

        TYPE SQL STATEMENT, PRESS ENTER

        ===>_

















        F3=EXIT F4=PROMPT F6=INSERT LINE F9=RETRIEVE F10=COPY LINE
        F12=CANCEL          F13=SERVICES   F24=MORE KEYS
```

Figure 10.5   The Interactive SQL Screen

BOO BOO BOX	COMMAND STARTSQL IN LIBRARY *LIBL NOT FOUND. If you misspell the STRSQL command, you will receive an error message similar to the one above. In this case the command was erroneously spelled STARTSQL. 　　　No harm has been done. To correct the error, simply type the command correctly (at the command prompt) and press the Enter key.

See Chapter 3 for a discussion of the function keys defined on the bottom of the Interactive SQL screen.

Keyboard Mappings: Depending on the terminal or work station used to access the AS/400, different keystrokes may be required to achieve the same system response. For example, accomplishing the task of "pressing function key one" may mean simply pressing the key labeled F1 or, as is the case with the TELEX 178 Display Terminals, holding down the Alternate (ALT) key and then pressing the 1 key. Consult your system administrator, instructor, or lab assistant for specific instructions.

CREATING THE DATABASE

The first step in using the AS/400 and SQL to implement the relational database model depicted in Figure 10.1 is to define the object that will be used to store the collection of tables to be created in support of the model. The CREATE COLLECTION statement defines this object. After proceeding to the Interactive SQL screen (described in detail in Chapter 3), enter the statement

```
===>CREATE COLLECTION SCHOOL
```

As the system creates your collection, it will keep you informed of its progress by flashing on the bottom of the screen messages about its work in building the paths and system files needed to support an SQL database.

BOO BOO BOX

JUNKANDMOR TOO LONG. MAXIMUM 10 CHARACTERS.

Entering a statement such as

```
CREATE COLLECTION JUNKANDMOREJUNK
```

will result in the above error message. To correct the statement, specify a collection name that has no more than ten characters in it.

TOKEN - WAS NOT VALID. VALID TOKENS: <END-OF-STATEMENT>.

Entering a statement such as

```
CREATE COLLECTION JUN---@@K
```

will result in the above error message. To correct the statement, specify a collection name that is composed of valid characters (A–Z, 0–9, and the underscore).

After you have defined the object that will be used to store the collection of tables, you must define the tables. The CREATE TABLE statement is used to define a database table. On the AS/400, a database table is a physical file that will store the actual user data. To continue building the SCHOOL database, individually enter the following statements:

```
===>CREATE TABLE SCHOOL/HOUSING
      (DORM    CHAR(10)  NOT NULL,
       STREET  CHAR(20)  NOT NULL WITH DEFAULT,
       CITY    CHAR(10)  NOT NULL WITH DEFAULT,
       STATE   CHAR(2)   NOT NULL WITH DEFAULT,
       ZIP     CHAR(5)   NOT NULL WITH DEFAULT)
```

> **TIP**   Use the Return key to move the cursor down a line on the screen when typing the statement; press the Enter key only after the entire statement has been typed.

> **TIP**   After entering the above CREATE TABLE statement, you can save yourself some typing on the next CREATE TABLE statement by using the retrieve function F9. With the cursor located at the prompt, press F9. The last statement executed (CREATE TABLE SCHOOL/HOUSING) will be displayed. Use the arrow keys to move the cursor to the appropriate locations, and type over the appropriate words.

```
===>CREATE TABLE SCHOOL/STUDENT
       (SID     CHAR(4)      NOT NULL,
        FNAME   CHAR(10)     NOT NULL WITH DEFAULT,
        LNAME   CHAR(15)     NOT NULL WITH DEFAULT,
        MAJOR   CHAR(10)     NOT NULL WITH DEFAULT,
        DORM    CHAR(10)     NOT NULL WITH DEFAULT)
```

> **BOO BOO BOX**   Since there is no statement that allows you to modify the structure of a table once it has been created, if you make a mistake in defining the table, you must delete (drop) the table and then re-create it correctly. See the discussion of the DROP statement in Chapter 4.

```
===>CREATE TABLE SCHOOL/TEACHER
       (TID     CHAR(4)        NOT NULL,
        FNAME   CHAR(10)       NOT NULL WITH DEFAULT,
        LNAME   CHAR(15)       NOT NULL WITH DEFAULT,
        SALARY NUMERIC(7,2)    NOT NULL WITH DEFAULT,
        DEGREE CHAR(15)        NOT NULL WITH DEFAULT)

===>CREATE TABLE SCHOOL/COURSE
       (CID     CHAR(6)     NOT NULL,
        SECTION CHAR(4)     NOT NULL,
        LOCATION CHAR(5)    NOT NULL WITH DEFAULT,
        TITLE   CHAR(15)    NOT NULL WITH DEFAULT)

===>CREATE TABLE SCHOOL/GRADE
       (SID     CHAR(4)      NOT NULL,
        CID     CHAR(6)      NOT NULL,
        SECTION CHAR(4)      NOT NULL,
        SCORE   NUMERIC(3) NOT NULL WITH DEFAULT)

===>CREATE TABLE SCHOOL/TCOURSE
       (CID     CHAR(6) NOT NULL,
        SECTION CHAR(4) NOT NULL,
        TID     CHAR(4) NOT NULL)
```

LOADING DATA INTO THE DATABASE

After using the CREATE COLLECTION and the CREATE TABLE statements to create the physical data structures that support our logical data model, you can load data into the structures with the INSERT statement. The UPDATE statement is used to correct mistakes or revise data; the DELETE statement is used to remove data that are no longer required to be stored in the database.

The INSERT statement loads data into a table that has been previously created with the CREATE TABLE statement. Figure 10.6 depicts sample data for the tables that were created in support of the SCHOOL database. The INSERT statement can be used to load these data into the database. Each INSERT statement entered will add one row of data into a table. To load the sample data provided in Figure 10.6 into the SCHOOL database, you will execute a series of INSERT statements.

Add data into the HOUSING table by entering these statements. (*Hint:* Remember to use function key F9 after you've entered the first statement.)

```
INSERT INTO SCHOOL/HOUSING
   VALUES ('LINCOLN', '111 CORNER AVENUE', 'FICTION', 'VA', '22555')

INSERT INTO SCHOOL/HOUSING
   VALUES ('MADISON', '222 THAT STREET', 'FICTION', 'VA', 22555')

INSERT INTO SCHOOL/HOUSING
   VALUES ('WASHINGTON', '333 THIS ROAD', 'FICTION', 'VA', '22555')
```

Check your work by entering the statement

```
SELECT * FROM SCHOOL/HOUSING
```

If errors are present, don't worry; you can correct them using UPDATE and/or DELETE (and then re-insert) statements, as discussed in the next section on updating data in the database.

Add data into the TEACHER table by entering the statements

```
INSERT INTO SCHOOL/TEACHER
   VALUES ('1010', 'PETE', 'NUMBER', 30000.45, 'PHD MATH')

INSERT INTO SCHOOL/TEACHER
   VALUES ('1020', 'SUE', 'ATOM', 41000.99, 'PHD PHYSICS')

INSERT INTO SCHOOL/TEACHER
   VALUES ('1030', 'JASON', 'DREAM', 55000.05, 'PHD LITERATURE')
```

Check your work by entering the statement

```
SELECT * FROM SCHOOL/TEACHER
```

Add data into the TCOURSE table (the intersection table that matches teachers to the courses they teach) by entering the statements at the top of page 123.

SCHOOL/HOUSING

DORM	STREET	CITY	STATE	ZIP
LINCOLN	111 CORNER AVENUE	FICTION	VA	22555
MADISON	222 THAT STREET	FICTION	VA	22555
WASHINGTON	333 THIS ROAD	FICTION	VA	22555

SCHOOL/TEACHER

TID	FNAME	LNAME	SALARY	DEGREE
1010	PETE	NUMBER	30000.45	PHD MATH
1020	SUE	ATOM	41000.99	PHD PHYSICS
1030	JASON	DREAM	55000.05	PHD LITERATURE

SCHOOL/STUDENT

SID	FNAME	LNAME	MAJOR	DORM
5000	JANE	DILLON	MATH	MADISON
5010	BILL	DOE	MATH	LINCOLN
5020	JOE	SMITH	ENGLISH	LINCOLN
5030	MARY	RIGHT	NURSING	MADISON
5040	KEVIN	GREAT	SCIENCE	WASHINGTON
5050	JOHN	JONES	NURSING	WASHINGTON
5060	JULIE	LEE	MATH	MADISON
5070	HENRY	ABLE	MATH	WASHINGTON

SCHOOL/GRADE

SID	CID	SECTION	SCORE
5010	MTH205	03N	85
5010	PHY200	01N	92
5000	MTH200	01N	98
5020	ENG100	01N	97
5020	MTH200	01N	75
5040	ENG100	01N	99
5040	PHY200	01N	98
5030	MTH200	01N	78
5060	MTH205	03N	89
5060	PHY200	01N	91
5060	ENG100	01N	98
5050	MTH200	01N	75

SCHOOL/TCOURSE

CID	SECTION	TID
MTH200	01N	1010
MTH205	03N	1010
PHY200	01N	1020
ENG100	01N	1030

SCHOOL/COURSE

CID	SECTION	LOCATION	TITLE
MTH200	01N	CT204	FINITE MATH
MTH205	03N	CT214	CALCULUS I
ENG100	01N	CG200	ENGLISH I
PHY200	01N	CT224	PHYSICS I

Figure 10.6 Sample Data

```
INSERT INTO SCHOOL/TCOURSE
    VALUES ('MTH200', '01N', '1010')

INSERT INTO SCHOOL/TCOURSE
    VALUES ('MTH205', '03N', '1010')

INSERT INTO SCHOOL/TCOURSE
    VALUES ('PHY200', '01N', '1020')

INSERT INTO SCHOOL/TCOURSE
    VALUES ('ENG100', '01N', '1030')
```

Check your work by entering the statement

```
SELECT * FROM SCHOOL/TCOURSE
```

Add data into the COURSE table by entering the statements

```
INSERT INTO SCHOOL/COURSE
    VALUES ('MTH200', '01N', 'CT204', 'FINITE MATH')

INSERT INTO SCHOOL/COURSE
    VALUES ('MTH205', '03N', 'CT214', 'CALCULUS I')

INSERT INTO SCHOOL/COURSE
    VALUES ('ENG100', '01N', 'CG200', 'ENGLISH I')

INSERT INTO SCHOOL/COURSE
    VALUES ('PHY200', '01N', 'CT224', 'PHYSICS I')
```

Check your work by entering the statement

```
SELECT * FROM SCHOOL/COURSE
```

Add data into the STUDENT table by entering the statement

```
INSERT INTO SCHOOL/STUDENT
    VALUES ('5000', 'JANE', 'DILLON', 'MATH', 'MADISON')
```

Repeat this statement to enter all of the following data for the STUDENT table:

SID	FNAME	LNAME	MAJOR	DORM
5010	BILL	DOE	MATH	LINCOLN
5020	JOE	SMITH	ENGLISH	LINCOLN
5030	MARY	RIGHT	NURSING	MADISON
5040	KEVIN	GREAT	SCIENCE	WASHINGTON
5050	JOHN	JONES	NURSING	WASHINGTON
5060	JULIE	LEE	MATH	MADISON
5070	HENRY	ABLE	MATH	WASHINGTON

Check your work by entering the statement

```
SELECT * FROM SCHOOL/STUDENT
```

Add data into the GRADE table by entering the statement

```
INSERT INTO SCHOOL/GRADE
     VALUES ('5010', 'MTH205', '03N', 85)
```

Repeat this statement to enter all of the following data for the GRADE table:

SID	CID	SECTION	SCORE
5010	PHY200	01N	92
5000	MTH200	01N	98
5020	ENG100	01N	97
5020	MTH200	01N	75
5040	ENG100	01N	99
5040	PHY200	01N	98
5030	MTH200	01N	78
5060	MTH205	03N	89
5060	PHY200	01N	91
5060	ENG100	01N	98
5050	MTH200	01N	75

Check your work by entering the statement

```
SELECT * FROM SCHOOL/GRADE
```

UPDATING DATA IN THE DATABASE

The UPDATE statement is used to alter the values of specific columns that exist in a table. The row or rows to be updated are specified with the WHERE clause. Omitting the WHERE clause causes the change(s) specified in the SET clause to be applied to each row of the table. On the AS/400, up to 32,768 rows may be updated in any single UPDATE operation.

For example, change the address of the MADISON dormitory from '222 THAT STREET' by entering

```
UPDATE SCHOOL/HOUSING
    SET STREET = '213 HALF STREET'
    WHERE DORM = 'MADISON'
```

The UPDATE statement is not restricted to changing the value of only one field (column). The SET clause may introduce a list of field names and values. For example, change the last name of a student and the student's major by entering

```
UPDATE SCHOOL/STUDENT
    SET LNAME = 'HILLS', MAJOR = 'ENGLISH'
    WHERE SID = '5000'
```

In defining values for the field(s) in the SET clause, you may include expressions as well as a literal. For example, raise the salary of all teachers by 20 percent by entering

```
              UPDATE SCHOOL/TEACHER
                  SET SALARY = SALARY * 1.2
```

The DELETE statement is used to remove unwanted rows from a table. The WHERE clause is optional, but if you do not include it, *all* the rows will be deleted! The WHERE clause restricts the deletion to only those rows that meet the search condition.

For example, delete the student HENRY ABLE from the database by entering

```
          DELETE FROM SCHOOL/STUDENT
              WHERE FNAME = 'HENRY' AND LNAME = 'ABLE'
```

QUERYING THE DATABASE

The SELECT statement allows you to interactively query the database for information. The result of entering a SELECT statement is a temporary table of information, which does not affect the data or the structure of the database table(s) referenced to generate it.

For example, to display information on the students in the SCHOOL database, enter

```
              SELECT * FROM SCHOOL/STUDENT
```

Review the data that you have entered for the other SCHOOL tables by successively entering the following statements:

```
              SELECT * FROM SCHOOL/HOUSING

              SELECT * FROM SCHOOL/TEACHER

              SELECT * FROM SCHOOL/COURSE

              SELECT * FROM SCHOOL/GRADE

              SELECT * FROM SCHOOL/TCOURSE
```

Armed with our knowledge of the SELECT statement (see Chapters 6, 7, and 8), let's respond to some requests for information that have arisen in reference to the data contained in the SCHOOL database.

1. What are the names of the students and what are their respective majors?
   Enter

   ```
           SELECT FNAME, LNAME, MAJOR FROM SCHOOL/STUDENT
   ```

2. In alphabetical order, list the names of the students and the dormitories in which they live.
   Enter

   ```
           SELECT FNAME, LNAME, DORM FROM SCHOOL/STUDENT
               ORDER BY LNAME, FNAME
   ```

3. Which students are majoring in MATH?
   Enter

```
SELECT FNAME, LNAME FROM SCHOOL/STUDENT
   WHERE MAJOR = 'MATH'
```

4. Which students live in the WASHINGTON dormitory?

   Enter

```
SELECT FNAME, LNAME FROM SCHOOL/STUDENT
   WHERE DORM = 'WASHINGTON'
```

5. Who are the students living in the LINCOLN and MADISON dorms?

   Enter

```
SELECT FNAME, LNAME FROM SCHOOL/STUDENT
   WHERE DORM = 'LINCOLN' OR DORM = 'MADISON'
```

   or

```
SELECT FNAME, LNAME FROM SCHOOL/STUDENT
   WHERE DORM IN ('LINCOLN', 'MADISON')
```

6. Who teaches the course entitled 'ENGLISH I'?

   Enter

```
SELECT TEACHER.FNAME, TEACHER.LNAME
   FROM SCHOOL/TEACHER, SCHOOL/COURSE, SCHOOL/TCOURSE
   WHERE TEACHER.TID = TCOURSE.TID AND
         TCOURSE.CID = COURSE.CID AND
         TCOURSE.SECTION = COURSE.SECTION AND
         COURSE.TITLE = 'ENGLISH I'
```

7. What was the average grade of the students in MTH200 Section 01N? Display the
   answer with a single decimal value.

   Enter

```
SELECT DECIMAL(AVG(SCORE), 5, 1) FROM SCHOOL/GRADE
   WHERE CID = 'MTH200' AND SECTION = '01N'
```

8. What was the highest grade received by a student enrolled in MTH200 Section 01N?

   Enter

```
SELECT MAX(SCORE) FROM SCHOOL/GRADE
   WHERE CID = 'MTH200' AND SECTION = '01N'
```

9. In alphabetical order, list the last names of the students, the classes they took
   (including name, section, and title), their grades, and the last name of the professor
   who taught the course.

   Enter

```
SELECT S.LNAME, C.CID, C.SECTION, C.TITLE, G.SCORE, T.LNAME
   FROM SCHOOL/STUDENT S, SCHOOL/TEACHER T, SCHOOL/GRADE G,
       SCHOOL/COURSE C, SCHOOL/TCOURSE X
  WHERE S.SID = G.SID AND
        G.CID = C.CID AND G.SECTION = C.SECTION AND
        T.TID = X.TID AND
        X.CID = C.CID AND X.SECTION = C.SECTION
  ORDER BY S.LNAME
```

THE SIGN-OFF PROCESS

To terminate your Interactive SQL session and return to the menu system of the AS/400 (from which you may log off the AS/400 system), simply press function key three (F3), as noted at the bottom of the screen (F3=EXIT). After you press F3, the system will respond with the EXIT INTERACTIVE SQL screen depicted in Figure 10.7.

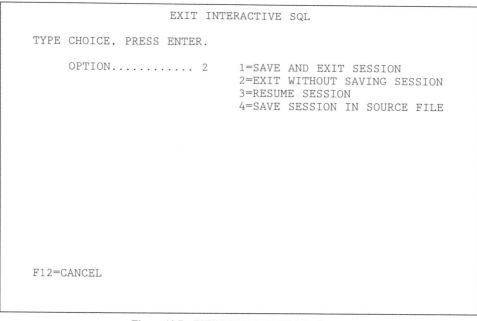

Figure 10.7 EXIT INTERACTIVE SQL Screen

Four options are presented. Choose option 2 by typing the number "2" and then pressing the Enter key. (If option 2 is the default on your system, you could just press the Enter key.) The menu screen from which you started your Interactive SQL session will appear.

> **TIP**   Option 2 is a clean way to exit. Don't worry; all of the collections, tables, and data created or stored are saved. What are not saved are the statements that were entered and the environment of the session as it was established by the parameters of the STRSQL command.

The AS/400 system is exited by choosing option 90 (SIGN OFF) from the MAIN MENU. If the MAIN MENU is currently displayed on the screen, type "90" at the command prompt and then press the Enter key.

> **TIP**   If a menu other than the MAIN MENU is currently on the screen, enter the command
>
>   ===>GO MAIN

The sign-off process may vary from this point. For example, at Northern Virginia Community College, the system responds with the screen depicted in Figure 10.8. Users on this system press the Enter key to end a session on the AS/400.

```
    mm/dd/yy              NVCC AS/400 ANNANDALE            hh:mm:ss

                    **   NVCC AS/400 SIGNOFF   **

    USERID: XXXXXXX       name of user


    TERMID: XXXXXX


                   LAST SIGNON:mm/dd/yy AT hh:mm.ss

                         USER TYPE: *PGMR






                   **   PRESS ENTER TO LOGOFF   **
```

Figure 10.8   AS/400 NVCC Sign-Off Screen

Appendix A

Normalization

THE ESSENCE OF NORMALIZATION

The relational database approach is based on storing and manipulating data in the form of logically related, two-dimensional tables. The ultimate goal of relational database design is to assemble a collection of tables that will support the information processing needs of users while providing a stable structure that will sustain the integrity of the data.

Normalization is a systematic approach for analyzing data and organizing the data into a group of logically related, two-dimensional tables. The normalization process progressively builds a collection of tables of an acceptable form. The normalization process classifies the analysis of data items into tables of first normal form (1NF), second normal form (2NF), third normal form (3NF), Boyce/Codd normal form (BCNF), fourth normal form (4NF), and fifth normal form (5NF). As a table is organized to meet specified conditions, it progresses from 1NF to 5NF.

Ensuring the integrity of the data through a stable data structure is the essence of the normalization process. A table advances from one normal form to the next when it meets certain conditions based on the constraints placed on the data (as defined by those who work with the data) and on the elimination of potential problems in retrieving or maintaining the data.

FUNCTIONAL DEPENDENCY

The acceptable form for a table depends on how the various columns (data items) are related to one another. If every value in column A has associated with it precisely one corresponding value in column B, then it is said that column B is *functionally dependent* on column A. In general, both column A and column B may refer to a single column or a collection of columns.

Functional dependency is directly related to the constraints placed on the data by the user. For example, the table in Figure A.1 depicts a collection of data for an organization keeping information on freelance photographers. The figure also lists constraints on the data. One constraint is that each photographer has a single phone number. The column PHOTOGRAPHER PHONE is said to be functionally dependent on the column PHOTOGRAPHER, because for each PHOTOGRAPHER there is exactly one corresponding PHOTOGRAPHER PHONE number.

PHOTOGRAPHER	SPECIALTY	MAGAZINE	PHOTOGRAPHER PHONE	ADDR	MAGAZINE PUBLISHER	PUBLISHER PHONE	ADDR
Joe Smith	Sports	Heroes	555-1111	12 Rd	Inky Inc	555-2222	1 Ave
	Fashion	Appeal			Inky Inc	555-2222	1 Ave
	Sports	Appeal			Inky Inc	555-2222	1 Ave
Mary Jones	Sports	Heroes	555-1212	10 St	Inky Inc	555-2222	1 Ave
	Civic	Heroes			Inky Inc	555-2222	1 Ave
Bill Law	Weather	Nature	555-1313	6 Ave	Printit	555-4444	3 Ave

Constraints:
1. Each photographer has associated with him/her a single phone number and address.
2. Photographers may have multiple specialties (i.e., take various kinds of pictures).
3. Photographers may be associated with multiple magazines.
4. Each magazine has a single publisher.
5. Each magazine may feature one or more specialties.
6. Each magazine publisher has associated with it a single phone number and address.

Figure A.1   Freelance Photographer Data and Constraints

A functional dependency may be represented symbolically as

```
PHOTOGRAPHER -> PHOTOGRAPHER PHONE
```

The expression may be read: "PHOTOGRAPHER functionally determines PHOTOGRAPHER PHONE." The column or columns on the left side of such an expression are referred to as *determinants*.[1] Determinants form the basis for keys; that is, all keys must be determinants.

For our purposes, a key is a column (or collection of columns) that uniquely identifies a row within a table. A candidate key is a proposed column (or collection of columns to be referenced together) that uniquely identifies each row of a particular table. Multiple candidate keys may exist, but at implementation time a particular candidate key is chosen as the key. There is no requirement that a determinant be a key, but if a column is a candidate key of a particular table, then all of the other columns within the table must be functionally dependent on that column.[2]

ACHIEVING FIRST NORMAL FORM (1NF)

The first step in systematically analyzing data and organizing the data into a group of logically related, two-dimensional tables is to make sure that multiple data values do not exist within a single row of a column. Consider the table depicted in Figure A.1, containing data on freelance photographers. Note that some of the rows have multiple values in their column positions; for example, Joe Smith has multiple specialties.

PHOTOGRAPHER	SPECIALTY	MAGAZINE	PHOTOGRAPHER PHONE	ADDR	MAGAZINE PUBLISHER	PUBLISHER PHONE	ADDR
Joe Smith	Sports	Heroes	555-1111	12 Rd	Inky Inc	555-2222	1 Ave
Joe Smith	Fashion	Appeal	555-1111	12 Rd	Inky Inc	555-2222	1 Ave
Joe Smith	Sports	Appeal	555-1111	12 Rd	Inky Inc	555-2222	1 Ave
Mary Jones	Sports	Heroes	555-1212	10 St	Inky Inc	555-2222	1 Ave
Mary Jones	Civic	Heroes	555-1212	10 St	Inky Inc	555-2222	1 Ave
Bill Law	Weather	Nature	555-1313	6 Ave	Printit	555-4444	3 Ave

Figure A.2   Example of 1NF Table for Freelance Photographer Data

Figure A.2 proposes a solution to this multiple values problem; it flattens each row by repeating data such as the photographer's name and phone number, thus creating several new rows. However, if the photographer name were the only column in the key to identify data on a photographer (keys are underlined in all figures), the table depicted in Figure A.2 would violate the relational rule that each row must be uniquely identified. For example, in Figure A.2 multiple rows of data are identified by the name Joe Smith.

In normalization terms, this is a problem of repeating groups. To remove the repeating groups and advance the table from unnormalized form to 1NF, we can simply propose a collection of columns (a candidate key) that, when referenced together, will uniquely identify each row. For example, 1NF may be achieved in our example by identifying

```
PHOTOGRAPHER NAME + SPECIALTY + MAGAZINE
```

as the candidate key.

Achieving 1NF is a step in the right direction, but it falls short of establishing a stable data structure for our data. Although the table depicted in Figure A.2 is 1NF, its storage of redundant data (such as the photographer's phone number and address) leads to a variety of potential problems in maintaining the data, not to mention excessive and unnecessary storage demands.

For example, in inserting or updating a row of data for JOE SMITH, we must be careful to enter the same phone number, address, and so forth, as in other rows with JOE SMITH data. One small data entry or update error could have JOE SMITH living at multiple addresses. Also, consider what happens if we delete BILL LAW from the database. Since information on the publisher PRINTIT is only contained in the row with data on BILL LAW, if we delete BILL LAW, we also lose all record of the publisher PRINTIT.

ACHIEVING SECOND NORMAL FORM (2NF)

Having achieved 1NF, our next step is to determine how we might adjust the table to eliminate some of these update anomalies. The massive amount of redundant data suggests that our table has columns in it that are not functionally dependent on our candidate key (PHOTOGRAPHER NAME + SPECIALTY + MAGAZINE). To achieve 2NF, we must eliminate any partial key dependencies that exist. That is, for any of the columns that are not a part of our candidate key, we ask the question: Are all of the elements of the key really required to identify the column, or can the column be identified with only a part of the key?

In Figure A.2, for example, must we know the SPECIALTY and the MAGAZINE associated with a photographer in order to identify the photographer's phone number and/or address? The answer is a definite no! Knowing only the PHOTOGRAPHER name is enough to lead us to PHOTOGRAPHER PHONE and/or PHOTOGRAPHER ADDRESS. Thus, the columns PHOTOGRAPHER PHONE and PHOTOGRAPHER ADDRESS are only dependent on one part of the candidate key, the PHOTOGRAPHER name.

We move from 1NF to 2NF by removing columns with partial key dependencies and placing them in a separate table with the part of the key that best identifies them. Figure A.3 advances our example to 2NF by creating two supporting tables (Tables 2 and 3), each of which stores data that are functionally dependent on the candidate key of the newly devised table. Note that only the non–candidate key columns were actually removed from the original Figure A.2 table. The part of the candidate key that was relevant to the extracted columns was, in essence, copied into the newly formed table. Thus, a table that is composed of only key columns (Table 1) remains a part of our collection of tables.

1

PHOTOGRAPHER	SPECIALTY	MAGAZINE
Joe Smith	Sports	Heroes
Joe Smith	Fashion	Appeal
Joe Smith	Sports	Appeal
Mary Jones	Sports	Heroes
Mary Jones	Civic	Heroes
Bill Law	Weather	Nature

2

PHOTOGRAPHER	PHOTOGRAPHER PHONE	ADDR
Joe Smith	555-1111	12 Rd
Mary Jones	555-1212	10 St
Bill Law	555-1313	6 Ave

3

MAGAZINE	MAGAZINE PUBLISHER	PUBLISHER PHONE	ADDR
Heroes	Inky Inc	555-2222	1 Ave
Appeal	Inky Inc	555-2222	1 Ave
Nature	Printit	555-4444	3 Ave

Figure A.3   Example of 2NF Tables for Freelance Photographer Data

Our newly devised collection of tables has helped alleviate some of the update problems. For example, updating data on photographers' phone numbers and addresses is easily accomplished because data on a photographer's phone number and address are stored in exactly one place (one row per photographer).

Although tables of 2NF are superior to tables of 1NF, we have not completely eliminated all possible update anomalies. For example, with reference to Figure A.3, consider the situation in which a MAGAZINE PUBLISHER publishes more than one magazine. Although the partial key dependencies were resolved, redundant data are still being stored and data entry/update problems persist. For example, data on the publisher Inky Inc are stored with data on each magazine it publishes. Further analysis of our data is required.

ACHIEVING THIRD NORMAL FORM (3NF)

We have already examined the relationship of the columns that were not a part of the candidate key to the columns that were a part of the candidate key and eliminated partial key dependencies. Our next step is to again examine the columns that are not a part of the candidate key. This time, however, we look at their relationships to each other (basically ignoring those columns that are a part of the candidate key for the moment). We are looking to eliminate transitive dependencies. That is, for each column that is not a part of our candidate key, we ask the question: Is this column better identified by another non–candidate key column or columns than it is by the candidate key column or columns?

In Figure A.3, for example, Table 1 is composed of all key items and thus, by definition, is in 3NF. Table 2 in Figure A.3 contains the non–candidate key columns PHOTOGRAPHER PHONE and PHOTOGRAPHER ADDRESS. To check for transitive dependencies, we ask the question: Does PHOTOGRAPHER PHONE better identify PHOTOGRAPHER ADDRESS than does the PHOTOGRAPHER name? The answer to this question is no. Next, does PHOTOGRAPHER ADDRESS better identify PHOTOGRAPHER PHONE than does the PHOTOGRAPHER name? Again, the answer is no. Thus, this table also is in 3NF. If we apply the same logical analysis to Table 3 in Figure A.3, we discover a transitive dependency and hence the cause of the update anomaly we noted earlier for Inky Inc.

As we proceed through the various permutations of our test question for transitivity, we soon discover that the answer is yes to two questions: Does MAGAZINE PUBLISHER better identify PUBLISHER ADDRESS than does the MAGAZINE name? And, does MAGAZINE PUBLISHER better identify PUBLISHER PHONE than does the MAGAZINE name? Note the transitive dependencies:

```
MAGAZINE -> MAGAZINE PUBLISHER -> PUBLISHER PHONE
```

and

```
MAGAZINE -> MAGAZINE PUBLISHER -> PUBLISHER ADDR
```

To eliminate the transitive dependencies, we create a new table that holds the transitive elements. The column or columns on which the elements are dependent become the candidate key. Figure A.4 illustrates the new table and the results of 3NF analysis. Note how 3NF analysis has produced a foreign key. As a result of 3NF analysis, MAGAZINE PUBLISHER becomes a candidate key in one table and a non–candidate key column in another table. Thus, MAGAZINE PUBLISHER is considered a foreign key in the table where it is not a part of the candidate key.

1

PHOTOGRAPHER	SPECIALTY	MAGAZINE
Joe Smith	Sports	Heroes
Joe Smith	Fashion	Appeal
Joe Smith	Sports	Appeal
Mary Jones	Sports	Heroes
Mary Jones	Civic	Heroes
Bill Law	Weather	Nature

2

PHOTOGRAPHER	PHOTOGRAPHER PHONE	ADDR
Joe Smith	555-1111	12 Rd
Mary Jones	555-1212	10 St
Bill Law	555-1313	6 Ave

3

MAGAZINE	MAGAZINE PUBLISHER
Heroes	Inky Inc
Appeal	Inky Inc
Nature	Printit

4

MAGAZINE PUBLISHER	PUBLISHER PHONE	ADDR
Inky Inc	555-2222	1 Ave
Printit	555-4444	3 Ave

Figure A.4   Example of 3NF Tables for Freelance Photographer Data

ACHIEVING BOYCE/CODD NORMAL FORM (BCNF)

Up to this point in our analysis, we have measured candidate key columns against non–candidate key columns and non–candidate key columns against non–candidate key columns. Ensuring that our tables are of Boyce/Codd normal form (BCNF) involves focusing our attention on only those columns that compose candidate keys. For a table to be in BCNF, every determinant must be a candidate key. Reviewing a table to ensure that it is in BCNF is important when the table has multiple candidate keys that are composite and the columns making up the candidate keys overlap.[3]

Our freelance photographer example in Figure A.4 has only one candidate key per table and thus, by definition, is in BCNF. However, to better understand the concept of BCNF, consider the 3NF table depicted in Figure A.5, which stores data on employees and the projects they are completing. Two candidate keys, each composed of multiple columns, exist:

EMPLOYEE	DEPARTMENT	PROJECT
Joe	Accounting	A
Bill	Accounting	A
Mary	MIS	B

Constraints:
1. An employee works in only one department.
2. A department works on only one project.
3. A project may have one or more employees working it.

Figure A.5   Example of 3NF Table Not in BCNF

$$EMPLOYEE + DEPARTMENT \rightarrow PROJECT$$

and

$$EMPLOYEE + PROJECT \rightarrow DEPARTMENT$$

Knowing the EMPLOYEE name and his or her DEPARTMENT yields data on what project the employee is completing. Likewise, knowing the EMPLOYEE name and what project he or she is completing yields the DEPARTMENT to which the employee is assigned. Note that the columns making up the candidate keys overlap, as each key uses the EMPLOYEE column.

The constraint that a department works on only one project is highlighted by the determinant

$$PROJECT \rightarrow DEPARTMENT$$

The determinant PROJECT is not used by itself as a candidate key, and hence the table in Figure A.5 is not in BCNF. Figure A.6 illustrates how BCNF is achieved by decomposing the table in Figure A.5 into two tables.

EMPLOYEE	PROJECT
Joe	A
Bill	A
Mary	B

PROJECT	DEPARTMENT
A	Accounting
B	MIS

Figure A.6   Example of BCNF Tables for Data on Employees, Departments, and Projects

ACHIEVING FOURTH NORMAL FORM (4NF)

Although it is generally agreed that 3NF or BCNF is an acceptable level for a physical database, it is still possible that the collection of tables may harbor update problems. Returning to our freelance photographer example, note that Table 1 in Figure A.4 is less than ideal. The table is host to a great deal of redundancy. For example, the PHOTOG-RAPHER name is repeated for each SPECIALTY of the photographer, because a PHO-

TOGRAPHER may have more than one SPECIALTY. Likewise, the MAGAZINE associated with a PHOTOGRAPHER is repeated for each SPECIALTY of a PHOTOGRAPHER. The problem is one of multi-valued dependencies. Figure A.7 illustrates how 4NF is achieved by decomposing Table 1 into two tables.

1a

PHOTOGRAPHER	SPECIALTY
Joe Smith	Sports
Joe Smith	Fashion
Mary Jones	Sports
Mary Jones	Civic
Bill Law	Weather

1b

PHOTOGRAPHER	MAGAZINE
Joe Smith	Heroes
Joe Smith	Appeal
Mary Jones	Heroes
Bill Law	Nature

2

PHOTOGRAPHER	PHOTOGRAPHER PHONE	ADDR
Joe Smith	555-1111	12 Rd
Mary Jones	555-1212	10 St
Bill Law	555-1313	6 Ave

3

MAGAZINE	MAGAZINE PUBLISHER
Heroes	Inky Inc
Appeal	Inky Inc
Nature	Printit

4

MAGAZINE PUBLISHER	PUBLISHER PHONE	ADDR
Inky Inc	555-2222	1 Ave
Printit	555-4444	3 Ave

Figure A.7   Example of 4NF Tables for Freelance Photographer Data

ACHIEVING FIFTH NORMAL FORM (5NF)

Up to this point we have found that progressing through the normal forms entails decomposing a troubled table into two supporting tables. There are cases, however, when we cannot cure the ills of a table simply by decomposing it into two tables. Such a situation exists in our freelance photographer example. The constraint that a magazine may accept photographs with multiple specialties means that the relevance of SPECIALTY to MAGAZINE must be considered.

The solution proposed in Figure A.7 does not address this concern. Figure A.8 demonstrates the results of decomposing Table 1 from Figure A.4 into three subsequent tables of 5NF. Although the normalization process is a methodical approach to organizing data, it remains an intuitive process, dependent on the data constraints defined by those who work with the data.

1a

PHOTOGRAPHER	SPECIALTY
Joe Smith	Sports
Joe Smith	Fashion
Mary Jones	Sports
Mary Jones	Civic
Bill Law	Weather

1b

PHOTOGRAPHER	MAGAZINE
Joe Smith	Heroes
Joe Smith	Appeal
Mary Jones	Heroes
Bill Law	Nature

1c

SPECIALTY	MAGAZINE
Sports	Heroes
Fashion	Appeal
Sports	Appeal
Civic	Heroes
Weather	Nature

2

PHOTOGRAPHER	PHOTOGRAPHER PHONE	ADDR
Joe Smith	555-1111	12 Rd
Mary Jones	555-1212	10 St
Bill Law	555-1313	6 Ave

3

MAGAZINE	MAGAZINE PUBLISHER
Heroes	Inky Inc
Appeal	Inky Inc
Nature	Printit

4

MAGAZINE PUBLISHER	PUBLISHER PHONE	ADDR
Inky Inc	555-2222	1 Ave
Printit	555-4444	3 Ave

Figure A.8   Example of 5NF Tables for Freelance Photographer Data

ENDNOTES

1. David M. Kroenke, *Database Processing: Fundamentals*, *Design*, *Implementation* (New York: Macmillan Publishing Company, 1992), pp. 177–178.
2. C. J. Date, *An Introduction to Database Systems*, *Volume 1*, *Fifth Edition*, copyright 1990 by Addison-Wesley Inc., 1990, pp. 529–530. Reprinted by permission.
3. Ibid., p. 543.

QUESTIONS

1. What is normalization? Why is it of importance in dealing with relational data modeling?
2. What is meant by *functional dependency*?
3. What kinds of update or data entry problems exist in an unnormalized table?
4. What is a determinant?
5. What is a candidate key?

EXERCISES

1. Match the following:

_____ 1NF   a. Eliminate multi-valued dependencies.

_____ 2NF   b. Eliminate repeating groups.

_____ 3NF   c. Eliminate partial key dependencies.

_____ BCNF   d. Decompose into three tables.

_____ 4NF   e. Eliminate transitive dependencies.

_____ 5NF   f. Make every determinant a candidate key.

2. Transform the following table into at least 3NF.

ACCOUNT NUMBER	CUSTOMER NAME	CUSTOMER ADDRESS	INVOICE NUMBER	INVOICE DATE	BALANCE
2000	Smith	22 Elm Street	222	1/1/90	$500
			222	1/1/93	$700
			280	2/1/93	$245
1005	Jones	14 Baker Road	233	1/1/91	$620
			234	1/6/91	$200
1010	Doe	91 Oak Avenue	240	1/9/93	$160

Constraints:

   1. Account number uniquely identifies a customer.

   2. A customer may have one or more invoices.

   3. An invoice date and dollar balance are associated with each invoice.

3. Transform the following table into at least 3NF.

STUDENT NUMBER	STUDENT NAME	DORMITORY	DORMITORY ADDRESS	CLASS	PROFESSOR	GRADE
111	Smith	Lincoln	213 Oak St	Math I	Dr. Number	B
				Science I	Dr. Atom	A
222	Jones	Lincoln	213 Oak St	Math I	Dr. Number	A
3333	Doe	Madison	456 Oak St	English I	Dr. Dream	C
				Science I	Dr. Atom	C
				Math I	Dr. Number	C

Constraints:

   1. Student number uniquely identifies a student.

   2. Each student is assigned to a single dormitory.

   3. A student may attend one or more classes and earns one grade per class attended.

   4. A single professor is associated with a class.

Appendix B

Introduction to
the IBM AS/400

INTRODUCTION

Computers come in all shapes and sizes. Some computers require a large, environmentally controlled room; others fit into the palm of your hand. Computers are as diverse in purpose as they are in shape and size. From processing the information requirements of a business to playing games, computers have many uses.

A widely accepted classification scheme divides computers into three broad categories:

1. Mainframe computers
2. Mini-computers, or mid-range computers
3. Microcomputers, or personal computers

Mainframe computers are typically large machines that require environmentally controlled rooms in order to operate effectively. As their size might suggest, mainframe computers provide processing power and data storage capabilities that exceed those of the smaller sized mini- and microcomputers. For years, organizations have used large mainframe computers to support their data processing needs, although these computers are expensive and usually must be operated by personnel with special talents.

Advances in technology brought the mini-computer. Mini-computers offer many of the same computing services as mainframe computers. Like a mainframe computer, a mini-computer usually serves the information processing needs of multiple users. Although more limited in processing power and data storage capabilities, a mini-computer is a smaller and less expensive alternative to a mainframe. Effective operation of mini-computers, however, may still require a staff of computer programmers and technicians.

More recently, microcomputers have brought computing power to the general public. Although originally designed to serve the needs of a single user (at a time), microcomputers now often are interconnected and work much like their counterparts—mini- and mainframe computers. Microcomputers provide computing services in a user-friendly environment. Graphical interfaces and software designed for specific purposes allow computer users to focus on their data processing requirements without having to master the computer skills associated with computer programmers or technicians.

SYSTEMS APPLICATION ARCHITECTURE (SAA)

Today, organizations use computers in all three categories to meet their data processing needs. In fact, today's computing needs often require that data be passed from one category of machine to another. Unfortunately, communication and exchange of data between machines (particularly those in different categories) have proven difficult. IBM markets a wide selection of computers in each of the three categories. To satisfy the demand of users to interconnect the various types of computers, IBM introduced Systems Application Architecture (SAA) in 1987.[1]

SAA is an IBM standard for programming languages, user languages, and communications support among computer systems. The ultimate goal of SAA is to create a computing environment in which mainframe, mini-, and personal computers effectively communicate.

THE AS/400 COMPUTER

IBM introduced the Application System/400 (AS/400) in 1988.[2] The International Business Machines (IBM) Application System/400 (AS/400) is a mini-computer that provides computing services through the use of menus, a command line, a context-sensitive help service, and a prompting feature. In addition, the AS/400 supports the IBM Systems Application Architecture (SAA) connectivity scheme.

IBM mainframe computers, such as the System 370, feature a job control language (JCL) that programmers use to communicate their data processing requirements to the operating system. Like the mainframe products, the AS/400 has a control language (CL) that users may employ to control the operations of the AS/400 operating system. Like personal computers, the AS/400 features a command prompt. By entering a number that corresponds to a menu option or by entering one of the many available CL commands at the command prompt, users can direct the AS/400 operating system and control the operations of the computer.

Thus, although the AS/400 (like a mainframe computer) requires experienced computer professionals to set up and control its operation, in its daily use the AS/400 (like a personal computer) is supported by menus and a control language that provide the user with the computing power to directly address data processing needs.

DATA STORAGE SCHEME OF THE AS/400

The common denominator of storage on the AS/400 is the object. In simple terms, an object is something that takes up storage space. There are different kinds of objects. For example, a source program is an object, a data file is an object, and a library is an object. Each object has descriptive characteristics that define it. Descriptive characteristics include information on who created the object, who has rights to use it, the size of the object, and what is contained in the object, such as source code or data. When the AS/400 operating system works with an object, it associates the object with its descriptive characteristics.

The AS/400 operating system handles the details of how data are physically stored. Because users work with objects, they need not be concerned with these details. From a user standpoint, data storage on the AS/400 is based on the creation and manipulation of objects. An object of particular importance for data storage is the library. A library is a special kind of object that contains other objects.

There are three types of libraries:

1. A system library contains data associated with the AS/400 operating system.
2. A product library contains data used to support languages and utilities beyond those supported by the system library.
3. A user library contains user-defined data.

A system library is established on the AS/400 when the machine is installed. One or more product libraries also may exist. Product libraries support languages and utilities beyond those supported by the system library. For example, a system may have a product library that supports the RPG language. A system administrator establishes user libraries. Each user has a library.

Libraries contain files (recall that files also are objects). Data are collected into files. There are various types of files that are recognized by the AS/400 operating system. The data contained within a file may be instructions (for example, a source file) or the raw facts and figures that are to be processed (for example, a database file).

The database file has an additional element of file organization called the data member. In a database file, each data member is a collection of records. A record, in turn, is a grouping of fields. A field is the construct that holds the actual raw fact or figure to be processed.

A database file may exist as a physical file or as a logical file. A physical file contains actual application data, whereas a logical file is simply a redefinition of a physical file. A logical file allows for different views of the same physical file.

THE SIGN-ON PROCESS

Starting a work session on the AS/400 requires establishing communication between your work station and the AS/400. This process is referred to as the sign-on process.

Sign-on and sign-off processes will vary from one site to another. The process described here is that followed by the Computing Center at Northern Virginia Community College (NVCC), Annandale, Virginia. Although access procedures may differ, generally the menu screens generated by the AS/400 will be the same. Consult your system administrator or instructor to resolve any differences.

The first step in accessing the AS/400 is to obtain a user ID and a password from your instructor or system administrator. Next, locate a terminal or PC that can connect to the AS/400.

Figure B.1 depicts the initial screen you will probably see. This is not an AS/400 screen, but rather a screen used to provide access to the various systems available. To access the AS/400 system from this screen, you would enter the command "AS400" at the command prompt located near the bottom of the screen.

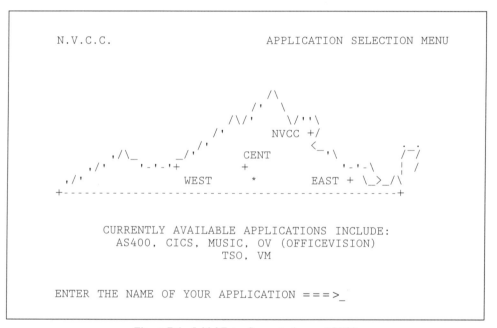

Figure B.1   Initial Entry Screen to Access AS/400

DEFINITION

The phrase **enter a command** means to type the desired command and then press the Enter key. Please note that the Enter key and the Return key do not have the same effect, unlike these keys on a personal computer. The Enter key signals the system to process what has been typed. The Return key (often symbolized by an arrow bent to the left) simply moves the cursor down a line. The Backspace key or arrow keys may be used to correct a typing error before the Enter key is pressed.

Figure B.2 depicts the resulting sign-on screen. Type your user ID, press the Return key (the bent arrow), type your password (the password is not displayed as you type it), and then press the Enter key.

```
                            SIGN ON

        NN      NN VV    VV CCCCC   CCCCC    SYSTEM.....: NVAS400
        NNN     NN VV    VV CCCCC   CCCCC    SUBSYSTEM..: QINTER
        NNNN    NN VV   VV CC       CC       DISPLAY....: NVHCF4
        NN NNNN   VV   VV  CC       CC
        NN  NNN   VV VV    CCCCC   CCCCC
        NN   NN   VVV       CCCCC   CCCCC


        AA      SSSSSS      ///    44   44   00000      00000
       AA AA    S           ///    44   44   00    00   00    00
       AA  AA   SSSSS       ///    44444444  00    00   00    00
      AAAAAAA        S      ///      44      00    00  00    00
     AA    AA        S  ///          44      00    00  00    00
     AA    AA   SSSSSS  ///          44       00000      00000


              USERID ................. _
              PASSWORD ..............


    ENTER USERID AND PASSWORD OR LEAVE FIELD BLANK FOR DEMO AND
    HIT ENTER
```

Figure B.2 AS/400 NVCC Sign-On Screen

	CPF 1107 - PASSWORD NOT CORRECT FOR USER PROFILE
BOO BOO BOX	Do not press the Enter key until you have typed both your user ID and your password. The Enter key signals the system to process what you have typed. If you type your user ID and then press the Enter key, the system will respond with the above error message. To correct the problem, press the Return key (Tab key on the PC), type your password, and then press the Enter key. The Return key does not signal the system to process an entry, but instead simply moves the cursor down a line.

THE AS/400 MENU SYSTEM

With the exception of the request to change your password (or to alter a user profile, a topic beyond the scope of this book), the AS/400 MAIN MENU screen is the first screen presented upon entry into the system. Figure B.3 illustrates the AS/400 MAIN MENU screen.

```
  MAIN                      AS/400 MAIN MENU
                                                  SYSTEM: NVAS400
  SELECT ONE OF THE FOLLOWING:

        1. USER TASKS
        2. OFFICE TASKS
        3. GENERAL SYSTEM TASKS
        4. FILES, LIBRARIES, AND FOLDERS
        5. PROGRAMMING
        6. COMMUNICATIONS
        7. DEFINE OR CHANGE THE SYSTEM
        8. PROBLEM HANDLING
        9. DISPLAY A MENU
       10. INFORMATION ASSISTANT OPTIONS

       90. SIGN OFF


  SELECTION OR COMMAND
  ===>_

  F3=EXIT F4=PROMPT F9=RETRIEVE F12=CANCEL F13=INFO ASSISTANT
  F23=SET INITIAL MENU
                           © COPYRIGHT IBM CORP. 1980, 1993
```

Figure B.3   The AS/400 MAIN MENU Screen

To select an option from the MAIN MENU, simply enter the corresponding number of the desired option at the command prompt

```
            SELECTION OR COMMAND
            ===>_
```

and then press the Enter key. For a detailed discussion of the AS/400 menu system and the MAIN MENU options and for directions on using these services, see Appendix C.

THE AS/400 COMMAND PROMPT

The AS/400 command prompt

```
            SELECTION OR COMMAND
            ===>_
```

found at the bottom of most screens displayed by the system, accepts far more than the numbers associated with menu options. User control of the AS/400 operating system is made possible through a powerful control language (CL). There are hundreds of CL commands that allow you to control the operations of the system. And, as with the DOS oper-

Note: Copyrighted screens in this chapter are used by permission of IBM Corporation.

ating system found on personal computers, some of these commands may be entered at the command prompt. For example, by entering the command

$$= = = >\texttt{STRSQL}$$

at the command line, you can access Interactive SQL.

> **T I P**   Press function key three (F3) to exit from Interactive SQL.

BUILT-IN HELP FEATURE

The AS/400 offers an on-line, context-sensitive help feature. When you request help, the AS/400 provides information relative to the current action. Information on how to use the AS/400 help feature is provided as a menu choice on the INFORMATION ASSISTANT OPTIONS menu. To reach the INFORMATION ASSISTANT OPTIONS menu, choose option 10 from the MAIN MENU or enter the command GO INFO at the command prompt. Help also may be accessed by pressing function key one (F1).

Keyboard Mapping: Depending on the terminal or work station used to access the AS/400, different keystrokes may be required to achieve the same system response. For example, accomplishing the task of "pressing function key one" may mean simply pressing the key labeled F1 or, as is the case with the TELEX 178 Display Terminals, holding down the Alternate (ALT) key and then pressing the 1 key. Consult your system administrator, instructor, or lab assistant for specific instructions.

THE AS/400 PROMPTING FEATURE

Along with providing a context-sensitive help service, the AS/400 offers assistance in command definition. If you can't remember command syntax, you may type part of a command and then press function key four (F4). You are prompted with a fill-in-the-blanks screen. Use of this feature is demonstrated in Chapters 4, 5, and 8 of this book.

THE SIGN-OFF PROCESS

The AS/400 system is exited by choosing option 90 (SIGN OFF) from the MAIN MENU. If the MAIN MENU is currently displayed on the screen, type "90" at the command prompt and then press the Enter key.

Sign-off procedures may vary. At Northern Virginia Community College (NVCC), the system responds with the screen depicted in Figure B.4. As the message on the bottom of the screen suggests, you would press the Enter key to end an NVCC session.

> **TIP** If a menu other than the MAIN MENU is currently on the screen, enter the
> command
>
> $$===>GO\ MAIN$$

```
   mm/dd/yy              NVCC AS/400 ANNANDALE              hh:mm:ss

                   **   NVCC AS/400 SIGNOFF   **

   USERID: XXXXXXX        name of user


   TERMID: XXXXXX


                  LAST SIGNON:mm/dd/yy AT hh:mm.ss

                        USER TYPE: *PGMR






              **   PRESS ENTER TO LOGOFF   **
```

Figure B.4   AS/400 NVCC Sign-Off Screen

SUMMARY

A computer can be classified into one of three categories: a mainframe computer, a mini-computer (mid-range computer), or a microcomputer (personal computer). The IBM Application System/400 (AS/400) is a mini-computer that was introduced by IBM in 1988.

The AS/400 provides its computing services through the use of menus, a command line, a context-sensitive help service, and a prompting feature. In addition, the AS/400 responds to the demand for integration by supporting IBM's SAA connectivity scheme.

Sign-on and sign-off processes will vary, but in general one must obtain a user ID and a password. After you have connected to the AS/400, the MAIN MENU screen will be displayed. The AS/400 MAIN MENU screen presents a list of options and a command prompt. At the command prompt, you may enter the number of an item from the list on the screen or enter a control language (CL) command.

ENDNOTES

1. "News 3X/400 Timeline," *NEWS 3X/400* (July 1992): insert following page A-48.
2. Ibid.

QUESTIONS

1. Of what benefit is IBM's Systems Application Architecture (SAA)?
2. What features of the IBM AS/400 distinguish it from other computer systems?
3. Does it make a difference whether one accesses the AS/400 system using a personal computer work station or an IBM 3270 series terminal?

EXERCISES

1. Secure a user ID and the corresponding password. Locate a terminal or work station that has access to an AS/400 and sign on to the AS/400 system, using your user ID and password.
2. Upon display of the MAIN MENU screen, practice working with the context-sensitive help feature to learn about each of the menu options. For example, to find out about the first menu option, type "1" at the command prompt and then press function key one (F1). **IMPORTANT:** Do not press the Enter key! After reviewing the information provided and returning to the MAIN MENU screen, use the backspace key to remove the 1. Then type "2" and press F1. Repeat this process until you have reviewed information on each of the options on the MAIN MENU.
3. Select the second option on the MAIN MENU by entering a "2" at the command prompt. (It's okay now to press the Enter key.) After reading over the options available on the menu screen that results, return to the MAIN MENU by using the GO command

   ```
   ====>GO MAIN
   ```

4. Sign off the AS/400 system.

Appendix C

Options Available
on the AS/400

GENERAL FORM OF AN AS/400 MENU

All of the AS/400 menu screens have the same general form. Figure C.1 depicts the AS/400 MAIN MENU screen. This screen is typical of the menu screens that you will see.

```
 MAIN                          AS/400 MAIN MENU
                                                      SYSTEM: NVAS400
 SELECT ONE OF THE FOLLOWING:

         1. USER TASKS
         2. OFFICE TASKS
         3. GENERAL SYSTEM TASKS
         4. FILES, LIBRARIES, AND FOLDERS
         5. PROGRAMMING
         6. COMMUNICATIONS
         7. DEFINE OR CHANGE THE SYSTEM
         8. PROBLEM HANDLING
         9. DISPLAY A MENU
        10. INFORMATION ASSISTANT OPTIONS

        90. SIGN OFF

 SELECTION OR COMMAND
 ===>_

 F3=EXIT F4=PROMPT F9=RETRIEVE F12=CANCEL F13=INFO ASSISTANT
 F23=SET INITIAL MENU
                              © COPYRIGHT IBM CORP. 1980, 1993
```

Figure C.1   The AS/400 MAIN MENU Screen

Note: Copyrighted screens in this chapter are used by permission of IBM Corporation.

In the upper left-hand corner of the screen is the system name of the menu (MAIN). The top center of the screen displays the descriptive title of the screen (AS/400 MAIN MENU). The middle part of the screen contains a numbered list of options. Under the list of options and near the bottom of the screen is the command prompt (===>_). Below the command prompt, at the bottom of the screen, is a list of function keys that are available for your use—for example, F3=EXIT.

D E F I N I T I O N

Function keys are unique keys. Rather than produce a character on the screen or control the movement of the cursor, a **function key** performs a programmed action. On some keyboards, such as PC keyboards, the keys are labeled F1, F2, and so forth. On other keyboards, such as the Telex 178 and IBM 3270 series keyboards, the keys are labeled PF1, PF2, and so forth.

To select an option from the menu, you simply type the number corresponding to the option you desire at the command prompt and then press the Enter key. Submenu and fill-in-the-blanks screens often appear to assist you in completing your work.

As an example, let's look at how you can use the menu system to change your password. Changing your password is offered as an option on the USER TASKS menu. To work with USER TASKS (the first option on the MAIN MENU), type a "1" at the command prompt and then press the Enter key.

```
  USER                        USER TASKS
                                            SYSTEM: NVAS400
  SELECT ONE OF THE FOLLOWING:

      1. DISPLAY OR CHANGE YOUR JOB
      2. DISPLAY MESSAGES
      3. SEND A MESSAGE
      4. SUBMIT A JOB
      5. WORK WITH YOUR SPOOLED OUTPUT FILES
      6. WORK WITH YOUR BATCH JOBS
      7. DISPLAY OR CHANGE YOUR LIBRARY LIST
      8. CHANGE YOUR PASSWORD
      9. CHANGE YOUR PROFILE

     60. MORE USER TASK OPTIONS

     90. SIGN OFF

  SELECTION OR COMMAND
  ===>_

  F3=EXIT F4=PROMPT F9=RETRIEVE F12=CANCEL F13=INFO ASSISTANT
  F16=AS/400 MAIN MENU
                        © COPYRIGHT IBM CORP. 1980, 1993
```

Figure C.2   The USER TASKS Menu Screen

Figure C.2 illustrates the USER TASKS menu that will appear. Note that the USER TASKS menu screen has the same general form as the AS/400 MAIN MENU screen. To change your password, select option 8 by typing an "8" at the command prompt and then pressing the Enter key.

Figure C.3 illustrates the CHANGE PASSWORD fill-in-the-blanks screen that results. To return to the USER TASKS menu without changing your password, press function key twelve (F12=CANCEL).

> **TIP**   To return to the MAIN MENU screen, press function key sixteen (F16) or enter the command GO MAIN at the command prompt.

```
                        CHANGE PASSWORD

        PASSWORD LAST CHANGED ..........: mm/dd/yy

        TYPE CHOICES, PRESS ENTER.

        CURRENT PASSWORD ............ _

        NEW PASSWORD ...............

        NEW PASSWORD (TO VERIFY) ....




        F3=EXIT     F12=CANCEL
```

Figure C.3   Fill-in-the-Blanks CHANGE PASSWORD Screen

OPTIONS ON THE AS/400 MAIN MENU

As Figure C.1 illustrates, the AS/400 MAIN MENU offers you eleven choices. The first ten are numbered 1 to 10. The last option, the sign-off option, is number 90. With the exception of the sign-off option and the display-a-menu option, each of the options, when selected, provides a submenu of options. The ten options of the MAIN MENU and their purpose are as follows.

1. USER TASKS   Offers a submenu of tasks that are
                                     related to your own work.

These tasks include changing your password, working with your user profile, displaying or changing your library list, and submitting or working with batch jobs.

2. OFFICE TASKS

Offers a submenu of tasks that support office activities such as working with documents, folders, and electronic mail. Decision support tasks related to database processing are supported (Interactive SQL is accessed from the DECISION SUPPORT option on this menu).

3. GENERAL SYSTEM TASKS

Offers a submenu of tasks that support your work with all jobs on the system. Displaying system operator messages, using communication devices, and backup and recovery of files are some of the services offered.

4. FILES, LIBRARIES, AND FOLDERS

Offers a submenu of tasks that allow you to work with files, libraries, folders, and host system tasks for AS/400 PC support.

5. PROGRAMMING

Offers a submenu of tasks that support your work as a programmer. Programmer utilities, language debuggers, and the SQL precompiler are some of the services offered.

6. COMMUNICATIONS

Offers a submenu of tasks that support your establishing and maintaining your communications network.

7. DEFINE OR CHANGE THE SYSTEM

Offers a submenu of tasks that allow you to configure and install licensed programs and hardware products. In addition, menu options are available to display and/or change system values.

8. PROBLEM HANDLING

Offers a submenu of tasks that provide you with support in working with general system problems.

9. DISPLAY A MENU

Presents a fill-in-the-blanks screen where you identify the system name of a menu with which you wish to work.

10. INFORMATION ASSISTANT OPTIONS
(USER SUPPORT AND EDUCATION
on an early version of the AS/400 system)

Offers a submenu of tasks that pro
vide information on problem handling, how to use the help system,
and how to use commands, as well
as an on-line tutorial.

90. SIGN OFF

The exit door. Select it to terminate
your work session on the AS/400.

FUNCTION KEYS

Under the command prompt, at the bottom of each menu screen, is a list of function keys
and their purposes. The purpose of a function key remains the same throughout the various screens. The function keys described on the MAIN MENU and their purposes are as
follows:

F3=EXIT

Ends the current action and returns
you to the screen from which you
started the action.

F4=PROMPT

Provides assistance in entering or
selecting a command.

F9=RETRIEVE

Brings up the last command you
entered on the command line. By
repeatedly pressing this function
key, you can bring back previously
entered commands, going back one
command with each press of the
function key.

F12=CANCEL

Cancels the current display or menu
and returns you to the previous display or menu.

F13=INFORMATION ASSISTANT
(USER SUPPORT
on an early version of the AS/400 system)

Displays the INFORMATION
ASSISTANT menu. Pressing this
function key is similar to entering
the command GO INFO. (On earlier releases of the AS/400 system,
F13 corresponded to USER SUP-
PORT, which displayed a USER
SUPPORT AND EDUCATION
menu that could also be reached
with the command GO SUPPORT.)

F23=SET INITIAL MENU

Changes the first menu you see when you sign on to the AS/400. When you press this key you are modifying your user profile, which (among other things) defines which menu will be initially displayed upon sign-on to the system.

Submenu screens, which are accessed via the MAIN MENU, list the same function keys as the main menu, except that function key sixteen appears instead of function key twenty-three.

F16=SYSTEM MAIN MENU

Returns to the AS/400 MAIN MENU.

Not listed on the bottom of the screen, but also available, are the following:

F1=HELP

Provides information on using the system. The information displayed depends on where you are when you request help. Help is context-sensitive, which means that the information provided is related to the ongoing action.

F7=SCROLL BACKWARD

Returns to the previous screen. When working with multiple screens of information, you will see the note "MORE. . ." on the bottom right side of the screen. As you read through the multiple screens, use this function key to get back to the previous screen.

F8=SCROLL FORWARD

Advances to the following screen. When working with multiple screens of information, you will see the note "MORE. . ." on the bottom right side of the screen. Use this function key to go on to the next screen of information.

Many of the screens presented during an Interactive SQL session offer additional function keys. Chapter 3 discusses starting an Interactive SQL session and using these additional function keys.

CONTROL LANGUAGE COMMANDS

Your control of the AS/400 operating system extends beyond the use of menu and fill-in-the-blanks screens. The AS/400 control language (CL) commands allow you to control the operations of the system and enter programs without using the menu system. Discussing the coding of programs using AS/400 CL is beyond the scope of this book. Instead, we will focus our attention on only a few of the many AS/400 CL commands that may be entered at the command prompt.

The AS/400 command prompt

```
SELECTION OR COMMAND
===>_
```

found at the bottom of all menu screens, accepts far more than the numbers associated with menu options.

For example, you may gain immediate access to any AS/400 menu by executing the GO command. Simply follow the command GO with the system name of the menu you desire. For example, by entering the command

```
===>GO DECISION
```

at the command line, you access the DECISION SUPPORT menu without having to access the OFFICE TASKS menu.

> **TIP**   Control language commands may be entered on any screen that has a command prompt.

The system name and descriptive name of each of the submenus that correspond to the MAIN MENU options appear in Table C.1.

TABLE C.1 SUBMENUS

System Name	Descriptive Name
USER	1. USER TASKS
OFCTSK	2. OFFICE TASKS
SYSTEM	3. GENERAL SYSTEM TASKS
DATA	4. FILES, LIBRARIES, AND FOLDERS
PROGRAM	5. PROGRAMMING
CMN	6. COMMUNICATIONS
DEFINE	7. DEFINE OR CHANGE THE SYSTEM
PROBLEM	8. PROBLEM HANDLING
——	9. DISPLAY A MENU
INFO (SUPPORT)	10. INFORMATION ASSISTANT OPTIONS (USER SUPPORT AND EDUCATION in early versions of AS/400)
——	90. SIGN OFF

> **TIP** Enter the command GO MAJOR to receive a listing of the major command groups. From this listing you may identify additional commands of interest.

Perhaps the most important CL command with which you should be familiar is the STRSQL command. The STRSQL command starts an Interactive SQL session. Details on the syntax and use of the STRSQL command are provided in Chapter 3.

SUMMARY

All of the AS/400 menu screens have the same general form. The upper left-hand corner of the screen displays the system name of the menu; the top center of the screen displays the descriptive title of the screen; the middle part of the screen contains a numbered list of options; under the list of options and near the bottom of the screen is the command prompt; below the command prompt, at the bottom of the screen, is a list of function keys that are available for your use.

The AS/400 MAIN MENU itself offers you eleven choices: (1) USER TASKS, (2) OFFICE TASKS, (3) GENERAL SYSTEM TASKS, (4) FILES, LIBRARIES, AND FOLDERS, (5) PROGRAMMING, (6) COMMUNICATIONS, (7) DEFINE OR CHANGE THE SYSTEM, (8) PROBLEM HANDLING, (9) DISPLAY A MENU, (10) INFORMATION ASSISTANT, and (11) SIGN OFF (which is numbered 90 on the screen). With the exception of the sign-off option and the display-a-menu option, each of the options, when selected, provides a submenu of options.

Your control of the AS/400 operating system extends beyond the use of menu and fill-in-the-blanks screens. AS/400 CL commands allow you to control the operations of the system. You may gain immediate access to any AS/400 menu by executing the GO command. Perhaps the most important CL command is the STRSQL command, which starts an Interactive SQL session.

QUESTIONS

1. Describe the general form of an AS/400 menu screen.
2. What are the function keys? Is there a difference between F1 and PF1?
3. What is the purpose of function key one (F1)?

EXERCISES

1. Locate a terminal or work station that has access to an AS/400, and sign on to the AS/400 system.

2. Upon display of the MAIN MENU screen, choose the appropriate option(s) and change your password.

| **TIP** | Work with the first option on the MAIN MENU. |

3. Chart, three levels deep, the menu options available to you. Begin by writing down the options available to you on the MAIN MENU. When presented with a nonmenu screen (for example, a fill-in-the-blanks screen), simply return to the menu where you were last working.

| **TIP** | Use F12=CANCEL to return to a previous menu. |

4. Sign off the AS/400 system.

Index

A

application, 16
attribute, 3–4
AVG function, 80, 82, 86–87

B

base table, 12, 56
BCNF, 5, 13, 129, 134–135
BETWEEN predicate, 75, 77

C

candidate key, 5, 130–135
Codd, 2, 5, 11, 13
collection, 20–22, 32, 37, 41–44, 49, 52, 55, 61, 104, 119
column, 3–5, 8–9, 11–12, 18–23, 32, 45, 46, 50, 55, 58–59, 62, 65–66, 71–73, 83, 86, 89, 92, 95, 104, 107, 109, 124, 129–135
command prompt, 26, 49–50, 62, 67, 97, 111, 115, 118, 142, 144, 146, 149–150, 154–155

COMMENT ON statement, 20, 22–23
COMMIT statement, 20, 22–23, 32
control language (CL), 26, 62, 101–102, 111, 113, 140, 144, 146, 154–155
COUNT function, 80, 82, 87
CREATE COLLECTION statement, 20, 22–23, 41–43, 56, 58, 119, 121
CREATE INDEX statement, 20, 22–23, 54–56
CREATE TABLE statement, 20, 22–23, 45–50, 56, 58, 119–121
CREATE VIEW statement, 20, 22–23, 51–53, 56, 58

D

data entity, 7
data file, 1, 12–13, 141
data item, 3, 5, 8, 129
data model, 40, 56
  hierarchical, 40–41, 56
  network, 40–41, 56
  relational, 2, 4, 13, 40–42, 56, 91, 114–115, 119
data type, 3–4, 45, 46, 49–50, 73, 83, 86